Spanish Phonetics and Phonemics

Spanish Phonetics and Phonemics

Second Edition

by

HANS-JÖRG BUSCH

MEGHAN FRANCES DABKOWSKI

TOM LATHROP †

DOWNLOAD AUDIO AND

ANCILLARIES AT

www.LinguaTextBooks.com

LINGUATEXT

NEWARK DELAWARE

For Tom Lathrop, who had the idea to write this phonetics and phonemics textbook and who was the lead author of the first edition.
We miss you.

103 Walker Way
Newark, Delaware 19711 USA
(302) 453-8695

www.LinguaTextBooks.com

Manufactured in the United States of America

ISBN: 978-0-942566-66-6 (PB)

Table of Contents

Preface to the second edition

If this is your first experience with a course of a linguistics nature, most everything will be new to you: new terminology, new concepts, and particularly, new language sounds to master. But not to worry: we have a lot of experience teaching Spanish pronunciation to American students at the college level, and we also remember what it was like when we were learning this material ourselves.

This is the second edition of "Spanish Phonetics and Phonemics", which has been completely revised and updated. In the preface of the first edition from 2006, Thomas Lathrop, who had the idea to write this textbook and who was the lead author of the first edition, wrote the following:

> We cannot emphasize enough how important it is to pronounce well. ... Mastering pronunciation is quite a bit like mastering a musical instrument. You can learn enough about playing the guitar in a semester, enough to accompany yourself in a number of songs, but to play at the level of a concert musician or as a studio player requires many years of lessons and practice.

In the current edition, the intention to help you acquire a good pronunciation and give you all the tools to gain an understanding of the production and organization of the sounds in Spanish, has not changed at all. Furthermore, we have also continued in the current edition Tom Lathrop's philosophy and guiding principle which consisted in not overly complicating the description with unnecessary linguistic terminology and offer a useful, simple but comprehensive guide of Spanish phonetics and phonemics.

Since 2006, many students have used this book. Many of them became Spanish teachers themselves and now help their students acquire a good pronunciation. Tom Lathrop passed in February of 2014, and we want to continue his legacy. At the same time, we have updated the book and integrated the experiences that we accumulated in teaching with the first edition.

As we did in the first edition, we would like to thank Dora Marín and Alberto Delgado, both natives from Colombia, who read and recorded the exercises that come with this book. Furthermore, we thank Aurelia Río who read the text "La Guantanamera".

Please do not hesitate to contact one of the authors in case you have a suggestion or comment. Our email addresses are *mdabkows@udel.edu* and *leipzig@udel.edu*.

Meghan Frances Dabkowski

Hans-Jörg Busch

Newark, DE

2022

Introduction

This book is about the **PHONETICS** and **PHONEMICS** of Spanish. Phonetics is a linguistic discipline that deals with all the sounds that speakers produce in a specific language, and their acoustic, articulatory, and auditory characteristics. However, not all sounds and sound variations in a language are used to distinguish the meaning of the words that exist in this language. For example, some Spanish speakers pronounce the **j** in the word **caja** with a lot of friction, like ['ka.xa]; others use aspiration and say ['ka.ha]. Still, both refer to the same thing: `a box`. On the other hand, a single or multiple vibrations of the **r** in **pero** and **perro** clearly marks the different meaning of these words. The linguistic discipline that reduces the inventory of all the possible sounds that exist in a language to just those that are used to distinguish different meanings, is called **PHONEMICS** or **PHONOLOGY**. These differences or distinctive features define the concept of **PHONEMES** or **FAMILIES OF SOUNDS**. The number of sounds in a language that are used is limited and the number of phonemes is even more restricted.

Even though the goal of this book is to make you more familiar with the sounds of Spanish and how to pronounce them, we decided to begin his book with a chapter on **ORTHOGRAPHY**, the discipline that deals with the written word or how sounds and families of sounds are written, because Spanish learners normally first see the written word and then ask how it is pronounced. (For Spanish native speakers it is the opposite: first they are taught how to speak the language and then they learn how to write it.) Compared to other languages such as English and French, for example, Spanish has achieved a stage where one family of sounds corresponds roughly to one letter in writing. Still, for etymological and historical reasons, as well as deep rooted traditions of writing, there are still cases where the same phoneme is written with different graphemes or letters. Examples are the sound

[x] that can be written with **j**, **g** or **x**, and the phoneme /b/ that can be written **b** or **v**. Spanish has also conserved the letter **h**, which is silent and does not represent any sound at all. These special cases are presented in the chapter about orthography.

Chapter 3, that deals with syllabification in Spanish, bridges the areas of orthography and phonetics. Word division at the end of a line in writing, for example, is part of orthography. A syllable in phonetics is considered the smallest prosodic or rhythmic unit, which can be a little different from a syllable in writing. This chapter only examines the phonetic syllabification at the level of words. Chapter 14 studies the division of larger phonetic units, such as phrases, clauses and sentences that are called **PHONOLOGICAL PHRASES**.

Knowing how to divide words and phrases phonetically and how many syllables there are is essential to determine where to stress a word and whether or not it is necessary to put a written accent, also called **TILDE** in Spanish. This is the topic of Chapter 4.

Chapter 5 describes the vocalic system of Spanish (and English).

Chapter 6 sets the foundation for the phonological and phonetic description of the Spanish consonants that follows in Chapters 7-13.

While Chapter 3 only describes the syllabification of single words and Chapter 4 the word stress, Chapters 14 and 15 examine the syllabification and the rhythm of larger prosodic units, that are called **PHONOLOGICAL PHRASES**, and that are roughly equivalent to all the words between two pauses or two periods of silence in speaking or between punctuation marks (periods, commas, semicolons, and other signs) in writing.

Chapter 16 describes the intonation of phrases and sentences, and how the intonation curves correspond to different pragmatic meanings.

While you are reading this, approximately 500 million people worldwide speak Spanish as their native tongue. According to the yearbook "El español en el mundo 2018", published by the Cervantes Institute, 7.6% of the world population in 2018 were native speakers of Spanish. In 21 countries, Spanish is the official language. Therefore, it is not surprising that there is a lot of regional and social variation, especially in how people pronounce words and phrases, but also in the use of vocabulary and grammar. In Chapters 6-13 we have only mentioned some of the most important differences. In Chapter 17 you can find a more detailed description of the concept of **VARIATION** and more specific examples.

Finally, Chapter 18 describes and offers some practice for the phonetic transcription of larger units.

Graphical conventions in this book

1. Basic and recurring linguistic terms, especially when they are introduced, are written with upper case letters and in **BOLD**, for example **PHONEME**; you can find them also in the glossary at the end of this book.
2. English examples or translations of Spanish examples into English (as well as examples from other languages) are written with `Courier New`.
3. Spanish examples, for example **caja**, are bolded.
4. Alphabet letters, for example **b**, the same as Spanish words, are bolded as well.
5. Sounds and phonetic transcriptions are written in square brackets, for example [b] and ['ka.xa].
6. **PHONEMES** are written with backslashes, for example /b/.
7. A period not only marks the end of a sentence but also the end of a syllable, especially in the phonetic transcription: **pa.ra.gua.yo** [pa.ra.'gwa.ʝo].

1
Basic terminology

The object of this book is the description and practice of Spanish pronunciation, which is the field of two linguistics disciplines, phonetics, and phonemics. The written language is the domain of orthography. All three disciplines are interdependent but have their own rules and tools.

Phonetics

Phonetics and phonemics both study the spoken language. **PHONETICS** is the more practical discipline that examines all the sounds of a language and their acoustic, articulatory, and auditive characteristics. These are all the differences that one can hear, for example between a [b] in **baja** and a [p] in **paja** or between a [g] in the word **hongo** and a [ɣ] in **hago**. If you pronounce the letter **g** correctly in the two last words, the first **g** sounds like the English **g** in `hunger`. The second one is much softer and can hardly be heard. (You can find a more detailed description in Chapter 8.) Phonetics also studies the connections between sounds and describes the smallest prosodic language units, the syllables. Furthermore, it describes the links between syllables (Chapters 3 and 14), intonation (Chapter 16) and the rhythm of statements (Chapter 15). Sounds are always written in square brackets, for example [ɣ]. In order to represent sounds in this book, we use the **INERNATIONAL PHONETIC ALPHABET** (see p. 19). This alphabet is also used to transcribe how words, phrases, sentences, and texts sound. Sounds are also called **ALLOPHONES**.

Phonemics

The more theoretical and abstract sister of phonetics is a discipline called **PHONEMICS** (or **PHONOLOGY**), which studies systems of sounds and their distribution patterns, and tries to reduce all the possible sounds to groups or **FAMILIES OF SOUNDS**, called **PHONEMES**, which are used to distinguish the meaning of two words, for example **baja** (third person present of **bajar**) and **paja** (Engl. `straw`). The sounds [b] and [p] in Spanish are clearly used to distinguish two different meanings. That is why we say that they belong to two different families, the family /b/ and the family /p/.

Families of sounds or phonemes

The tendency to pronounce words in a foreign language as if they were our native language is a major, and even very natural and almost unavoidable, stumbling block, but an even more serious problem deals with "families of sounds". Every language has its own set of families of sounds, which are series of sounds that are related phonetically, each one being used in a different phonetic circumstance. Native speakers of a language are typically unaware that there is any variation at all among these sounds. Look at the English **t**. The /t/ family in English has several variations. At the beginning of a word (and at the beginning of a stressed syllable), the **t** is accompanied by a puff of air which is strong enough to blow out a match, even when you whisper it: for example in `tick`. This is called **ASPIRATION** and is expressed in the transcription with the symbol [t^h]. If **t** is the second sound in a syllable, it is prononced with no puff of air: for example, in `stick`. (If you blow out a match when you shout `stick` it may be due to the hissing of the **s** and not to the aspiration of the **t**.) Normally, a **t** is articulated by first shutting off the flow of air with the tongue at the **ALVEOLAR RIDGE**, and then releasing it. At the end of a word, for example in `bat`, there is a complete occlusion of the **GLOTTIS**, that results in the allophone [ʔ], a glottal stop. In American English, the **t** between vowels is typically flapped, as in `get up!` This sound is similar to the simple **r** in Spanish, for example in the word **pero**, and is represented with the symbol [ɾ] in the transcription. In total, there are five variations of the same sound. If you use the same sound, the **t** of `tick`, all the time, and do not use any of the variations, you'll be perfectly understood (although some people might think your pronunciation is odd – which it would be) because you will have stayed within the same family of sounds.

How can you tell one family from another? If you substitute one sound for another and the word means the same thing (as we suggested with the **t**s), it's from the same family. If you substitute a sound for another and the word means something different, then the two sounds belong to different families. In English, we have three families of nasal sounds, one of the /n/, one of the /m/, and another of the /ŋ/ (in sing). In English, seen, seem and sing mean three different things; therefore, those nasal sounds are members of three different families.

In Spanish, an **n** assimilates –moves to the same point of articulation as– to the following consonant. The word **sin** in **sin dinero** is pronounced seen; it is pronounced seem in **sin bases**; and in **sin ganas** it sounds almost (but not exactly) like seeing. Those three sounds are members of the same family in Spanish because the three variations all mean the same thing: without.

Linguists often call these "families of sounds" **PHONEMES**. They are identified by characters placed in between slashes, for example /g/. Phonemes are names, not sounds. Since they represent a family of different sounds, they themselves have no phonetic value. This concept is easy to grasp if you think of a family of persons, for example the "Simpsons". The family name is written in between slashes: /Simpson/. The members of the family are [Homer], [Marge], [Bart], [Lisa] and [Maggie]. You can say": "Draw me a picture of [Bart] because he is an entity with face and form, but you cannot say: "Draw me a picture of /Simpson/," because /Simpson/ is just a name or a label that represents five quite different individuals. Another example is /General Motors/. You can not say: "Well, I think I'll go buy a /General Motors/," because that's the name of the company that produces vehicles from tiny cars to giant tractors. Instead, you would say: "Well, I think I'll go buy a [Cadillac]." What could be potentially confusing is that the same symbol is frequently used for the phoneme and one of its allophones (sounds), /n/ and [n], for example. Just tell yourself: "A phoneme is just a name, and the allophones, the members of the family, are the sounds themselves. A phoneme is an abstraction and never represents any specific sound."

The International Phonetic Alphabet

In the mid-1880, some British scholars at Cambridge University organized the International Phonetics Association. They realized that every letter of the Roman alphabet could represent several different sounds, not only in English, but within the range of world languages. They wanted to invent a set of symbols, each of which would represent a single discrete speech sound and would be valid for any language. They kept the letters of the Roman alphabet (each for a specific sound). In addition, they came up with around twenty-five graphical variations of these letters and approximately thirty diacritic symbols. (Written accents, for example, are diacritic symbols.)

Here are some problems that are easily overcome with the phonetic alphabet. Within English itself there are enormous variations. Just compare the different pronunciations of

a) **–ng–** in singer, finger and ginger;

b) the **g** in the following pairs of words that are spelled almost identically: forger, forget; anger, danger; eager, wager; laughter, daughter;

c) double **s** in possessions and assign;

d) **who–** in who, whole and whoa;

e) the **s** in house and houses;

f) **–ough–** in rough, trough, though, thorough and thought;

g) **–ear** in hear, heard, heart;

h) **–omb** in bomb, comb, tomb;

i) **–ove** in move, love and dove (the past of dive);

j) **–ice-** in police, justice, licorice.

See if you can pronounce each of these words in two different ways: wound, produce, refuse, polish, lead, present, object, invalid, row, does, sewer, sow, wind, number, tear, subject. Look at how you pronounce graduate in these two examples: I will graduate in June and I'll be a graduate student. The spelling of a word in English simply does not indicate its pronunciation accurately, and in order to read aloud, you need to know how the word is pronounced.

THE INTERNATIONAL PHONETIC ALPHABET (revised to 2020)

CONSONANTS (PULMONIC)

	Bilabial	Labiodental	Dental	Alveolar	Postalveolar	Retroflex	Palatal	Velar	Uvular	Pharyngeal	Glottal
Plosive	p b			t d		ʈ ɖ	c ɟ	k ɡ	q ɢ		ʔ
Nasal	m	ɱ		n		ɳ	ɲ	ŋ	ɴ		
Trill	ʙ			r					ʀ		
Tap or Flap		ⱱ		ɾ		ɽ					
Fricative	ɸ β	f v	θ ð	s z	ʃ ʒ	ʂ ʐ	ç ʝ	x ɣ	χ ʁ	ħ ʕ	h ɦ
Lateral fricative				ɬ ɮ							
Approximant		ʋ		ɹ		ɻ	j	ɰ			
Lateral approximant				l		ɭ	ʎ	ʟ			

Symbols to the right in a cell are voiced, to the left are voiceless. Shaded areas denote articulations judged impossible.

CONSONANTS (NON-PULMONIC)

Clicks	Voiced implosives	Ejectives
ʘ Bilabial	ɓ Bilabial	ʼ Examples:
ǀ Dental	ɗ Dental/alveolar	pʼ Bilabial
ǃ (Post)alveolar	ʄ Palatal	tʼ Dental/alveolar
ǂ Palatoalveolar	ɠ Velar	kʼ Velar
ǁ Alveolar lateral	ʛ Uvular	sʼ Alveolar fricative

VOWELS

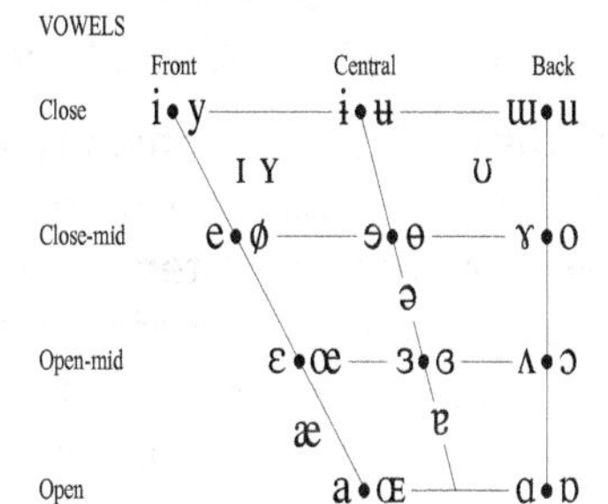

Where symbols appear in pairs, the one to the right represents a rounded vowel.

OTHER SYMBOLS

ʍ Voiceless labial-velar fricative

w Voiced labial-velar approximant

ɥ Voiced labial-palatal approximant

ʜ Voiceless epiglottal fricative

ʢ Voiced epiglottal fricative

ʡ Epiglottal plosive

ɕ ʑ Alveolo-palatal fricatives

ɺ Voiced alveolar lateral flap

ɧ Simultaneous ʃ and x

Affricates and double articulations can be represented by two symbols joined by a tie bar if necessary. t͡s k͡p

DIACRITICS

̥ Voiceless	n̥ d̥	̤ Breathy voiced	b̤ a̤	̪ Dental	t̪ d̪
̬ Voiced	s̬ t̬	̰ Creaky voiced	b̰ a̰	̺ Apical	t̺ d̺
ʰ Aspirated	tʰ dʰ	̼ Linguolabial	t̼ d̼	̻ Laminal	t̻ d̻
̹ More rounded	ɔ̹	ʷ Labialized	tʷ dʷ	̃ Nasalized	ẽ
̜ Less rounded	ɔ̜	ʲ Palatalized	tʲ dʲ	ⁿ Nasal release	dⁿ
̟ Advanced	u̟	ˠ Velarized	tˠ dˠ	ˡ Lateral release	dˡ
̠ Retracted	e̠	ˤ Pharyngealized	tˤ dˤ	̚ No audible release	d̚
̈ Centralized	ë	̴ Velarized or pharyngealized	ɫ		
̽ Mid-centralized	e̽	̝ Raised	e̝ (ɹ̝ = voiced alveolar fricative)		
̩ Syllabic	n̩	̞ Lowered	e̞ (β̞ = voiced bilabial approximant)		
̯ Non-syllabic	e̯	̘ Advanced Tongue Root	e̘		
˞ Rhoticity	ɚ a˞	̙ Retracted Tongue Root	e̙		

Some diacritics may be placed above a symbol with a descender, e.g. ŋ̊

SUPRASEGMENTALS

- ˈ Primary stress — ˌfoʊnəˈtɪʃən
- ˌ Secondary stress
- ː Long — eː
- ˑ Half-long — eˑ
- ̆ Extra-short — ĕ
- ǀ Minor (foot) group
- ‖ Major (intonation) group
- . Syllable break — ɹi.ækt
- ‿ Linking (absence of a break)

TONES AND WORD ACCENTS

LEVEL		CONTOUR	
e̋ or ˥	Extra high	ě or ˩˥	Rising
é ˦	High	ê ˥˩	Falling
ē ˧	Mid	e᷄ ˦˥	High rising
è ˨	Low	e᷅ ˩˨	Low rising
ȅ ˩	Extra low	e᷈ ˧˦˧	Rising-falling
ꜜ	Downstep	↗	Global rise
ꜛ	Upstep	↘	Global fall

Typefaces: Doulos SIL (metatext); Doulos SIL, IPA Kiel, IPA LS Uni (symbols)

Among foreign languages, the problem is compounded. **Ch** in English and Spanish is pronounced the same way (`channel`, **chiste**). However, in French and Portuguese, it's always like the **sh** in `ship` (Fr. `cache`, Ptg. `chave`); in Polish it's like the Spanish **j** (`chór = chorus`); in Italian it's like a **k**: `chianti`. The **ç** is like double **s** in French and Portuguese, but in Turkish it's like the English **ch** (`çok = very`).

The International Phonetic Alphabet is on the previous page and can also be found on-line at https://www.ipachart.com/.

Orthography

Orthography is the study of the spelling system of a language. The word is derived from Ancient Greek and means "correct writing".

In the evolution of humanity, writing and orthography are relatively recent phenomena, and there are many languages without writing systems. Alphabets, letters, and other orthographic symbols are only coarse instruments to represent the spoken language in writing. Think about it as two different codes, with their own characteristics. Both how we speak and how we write are the result of collective social and cultural conventions that are in a permanent process of transformation. Today, Spanish orthography has reached a high degree of stability and its rules are followed by all literate Spanish speakers. These rules are established by the language academies of the respective countries. Because Spanish is spoken in many countries – the 21 countries where Spanish is the official language + the United States of America, where approximately 50 million people speak Spanish – the national language academies work together in the *Asociación de Academias de la Lengua Española*. In 2010, this organization published the "*Ortografía de la lengua española*", that describes and prescribes how Spanish should be written today.

The Spanish alphabet and the phonetic alphabet

The current Spanish alphabet has twenty-seven (27) letters, one more than the English alphabet:

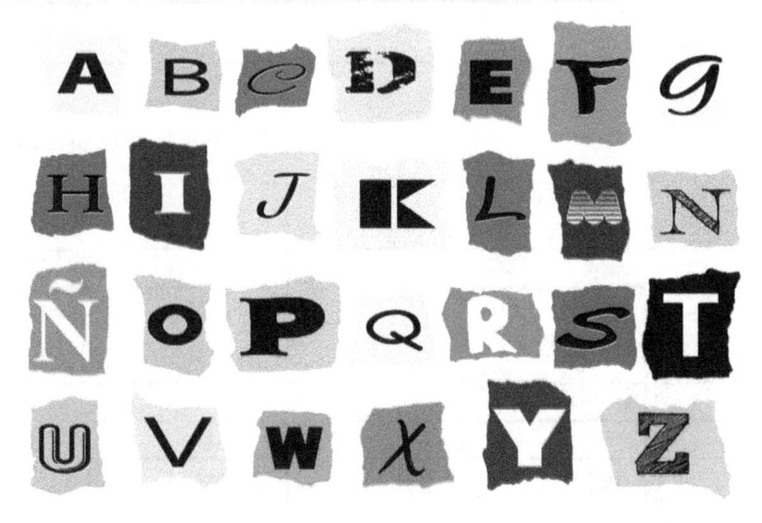

In addition, there are five (5) **DIGRAPHS**, combinations of two letters, **ch**, **ll**, **gu**, **qu** and **rr**. However, these no longer have their own section in the dictionary anymore as they did in the past. This means that **ch**, for example, can be found under the letter **c**, and comes right after the word **ceviche**.

In general, each **GRAPHEME** (each of the 27 letters and the 5 digraphs) represents one **PHONEME**, but several sounds. This implies that a letter can be pronounced differently in different positions within a word, in different parts of the Spanish speaking world and by different speakers.

Below, you can find a list of all the 27 letters and 5 digraphs, together with the names that the Spanish language academies recommend in the last edition of the *"Ortografía de la lengua española"* (see the bibliography at the end of this book), their phonemes and most frequent sounds that they represent.

letter	noun	phoneme	sound(s)
a	a	/a/	[a]
b	be	/b/	[b] ambos, boda [β] cabo

c	ce	/s/ /θ/ /k/	[s] cien [θ] cien (most parts of Spain) [k] coche
ch*	che	/tʃ/	[tʃ] chico
d	de	/d/	[d] dama [ð] cada
e	e	/e/	[e] era
f	efe	/f/	[f] fue
g	ge	/g/ /x/	[g] gato [ɣ] hago [x] gente
gu*	gue	/g/	[g] guerra
h	hache	Ø	[h] In general, it does not represent any sound in Spanish, but some dialects use aspiration
i	i (i latina)	/i/	[i] Lima [j] hielo, peine
j	jota	/x/	[x] caja
k	ka	/k/	[k] kilo
l	ele	/l/	[l] libro [l̪] alto [ʎ] colchón

ll*	elle	/ʎ/ /ɟ/	[ʎ] calle (northern Spain and some regions of the Andean mountain range) [ɟ] conllevar [ʝ] calle [ʒ] calle [ʃ] calle y otros
m	eme	/m/	[m] mamá
n	ene	/n/	[n] nada [ɱ] énfasis [n̪] antes [ɳ] encinta (only parts of Spain) [ɲ] inyección [ŋ] ancla
ñ	eñe	/ɲ/	[ɲ] caña
o	o	/o/	[o] ojo
p	pe	/p/	[p] papá
q	cu	/k/	[k] quena
qu*	cu u	/k/	[k] quena
r	ere	/ɾ/	[ɾ] pero
rr*	erre	/r/	[r] perro

s	ese	/s/	[s] mesa [z] mismo [s̺] mesa (only parts of Spain) [θ] mesa (only parts of Spain and Central America)
t	te	/t/	[t] tema
u	u	/u/	[u] uva [w] huelga, Ceuta
v	uve (ve)	/b/	[b] vaso [β] ave
w	uve doble (ve doble, doble uve, doble ve and doble u)	/w/	[w] Web
x	equis	/x/ /k/+/s/	[x] México [k] + [s] taxi
y	ye (i griega)	/ʝ/	[ɟ] mayo [ʒ] mayo [ʃ] mayo ... and others
z	zeta	/s/ /θ/	[s] Venezuela [θ] zumo (most parts of Spain)

* are not part of the modern Spanish alphabet

Consonants and vowels

The sounds [a], [e], [i], [o], [u] are **VOWELS** and the other sounds (except **GLIDES**) are **CONSONANTS**. What distinguishes them is that vowels come out of the mouth without passing through any obstruction. When you say "ah!" or "ee!" or any other vowel sound in any language, it flows out of your mouth unimpeded. A consonant, on the other hand, is a sound that has some impediment or obstacle that squeezes, stops, or reroutes the sound before it leaves your mouth. For the [p] sound, for example, the two lips prevent the air from leaving the mouth, they block it.

The sounds represented by the letters **u**, **i** – and in some cases also **y** – can be pronounced with some friction and without a constant articulatory position nor a stable acoustic quality. In that case, they are considered **SEMIVOWELS** or **GLIDES**.

Vowels and glides

We can distinguish:

1. the **LOW** and **MID VOWELS a, e, o**, also called **STRONG VOWELS**; and
2. the **HIGH VOWELS i** or **u**, also called **WEAK VOWELS**.

The five vowels **a**, **e**, **i**, **o**, **u** can be **FULL VOWELS**, and form, by themselves, the nucleus of a syllable: **mamá** [ma.'ma], **nene** ['ne.ne], **loro** ['lo.ro], **pipi** ['pi.pi], **lulú** [lu.'lu].

The combinations of **i** + **u** in the same syllable, as well as any combination of **a**, **e**, **o** with an **UNSTRESSED i** or **u** (without written accent) become **DIPHTHONGS** OR **TRIPHTHONGS**. In these groups, **a**, **e**, **o** always form the nucleus of the syllable, and **i**/**u**, in combination with them, become **SEMIVOWELS** or **GLIDES**. (They are called glides because they start the same as the full vowels **i**/**u** but move or glide towards the sound of the nucleus of the syllable. They do not have the constant articulatory position nor stable acoustic quality of full vowels.) If unstressed **i** + **u** occur in the same syllable, it is always the SECOND sound that becomes the nucleus. If **i** or **u** precede the nucleus, we call the combination **RISING DIPHTHONGS**, for example **ie, ue** or **ui**. If **i** or **u** follow the nucleus, we call them **FALLING DIPHTHONGS**, for example

ei or **eu**. Some linguists use different transcriptions for pre- and post-nuclear glides. In this book, both are written [j] and [w].

In writing, rising diphthongs can never start words in Spanish. That is why they are written with an **h** at the beginning: **hiato**, **hielo**, **hierba**, **hierro**, **hueco**, **huelga**, **huella**, **huele**, **huerta**, etc. Exceptions are loan words from other languages: **ion**, **iatrogenia**.

In the 2010 edition of the *"Ortografía de la lengua española"*, the Spanish Royal Language Academy (Real Academia de la Lengua Española, RAE) writes that the presence of an **h** between two vowels "does not prevent these vowels from forming diphthongs ... and that there are words, such as **de.sahu.cio**, **prohi.bi.ción** or **ahi.ja.do**, with an **h** in the middle, where the two vowel sounds are pronounced as diphthongs ..." (p. 197). Tom Lathrop, who lead the first edition of this book, always argued that even though the **h** was silent, it still represented a consonant, and that the words should be divided **pro.hi.bi.ción**, **a.hi.ja.do**, etc. Furthermore, if they were diphthongs, they should be pronounced [proj.βi.'sjon] and [aj.ʝa.ðo]. However, especially in slow and well-articulated speech, we can hear the pronunciation without diphthong: [pro.i.βi.'sjon] and [a.i.ʝa.ðo].

The semivowel [j], which is always written **i**, is different from the consonant [ʝ], that is written with the letters **y** or **ll**, because of the higher degree of friction and obstruction in the latter. (In Chapter 13 you can see that the letters **y** and **ll** are pronounced with different types of friction or as affricate sounds. In Chapter 17 about variation, you will find other pronunciations of **ll**.) Both can be at the beginning of words or syllables, for example in **llave**, **calle**, **yeso**, **cayó**, **haya**. There are no native Spanish words that end in **ll**. The letter **y** at the end of words represents the semivowel [j], for example in the words **hay** [aj] and **hoy** [oj]. However, if it is followed by another vowel, **y** is the consonant [ʝ], for example in **haya** ['a.ʝa].

The combination of three vocalic sounds in one syllable is called **TRIPHTHONG**. Triphthongs always start and end with an **i** or **u** (and in some cases with **y**, such as in the words **buey**, **guay** and **Paraguay**). When the **y** is followed by another vowel, then there is no triphthong. Here, the **y** is considered a consonant and starts the last or next syllable → **bue.yes** ['bwe.ʝes], **gua.ya** ['gwa.ʝa] and **pa.ra.gua.yo** [pa.ra.'gwa.ʝo].

Diphthongs

There are two types of diphthongs:

1. The combination of the **NUCLEAR VOWELS a**, **e**, **o** together with the **HIGH UNSTRESSED VOWELS i** or **u** in words like

   i + a, e, o — ['a.s**ja**] ha-c**ia**, [su.per.'fi.s**je**] su-per-fi-c**ie**, ['re.s**jo**] re-c**io**

   u + a, e, o — ['re.k**wa**] re-c**ua**, ['te.n**we**] te-n**ue**, [an.'ti.g**wo**] an-ti-g**uo**

   a, e, o + i — ['**aj**.re] **ai**-re, ['b**ej**n.te] v**ei**n-te, ['b**oj**.na] **boi**-na

   a, e, o + u — ['**aw**.to] **au**-to, ['d**ew**.ða] d**eu**-da, [b**ow**] b**ou** (Engl. `trawler`)

2. Any combination of **a**, **e**, **o** + **i** and **u** cannot be divided into two syllables, not in writing nor in speaking:

   WRONG: *te-nu-e ['te.nu.e]

   *de-u-da ['de.u.ða]

   *ha-ci-a ['a.si-a]

   RIGHT: te-n**ue** ['te.n**we**]

   d**eu**-da ['d**ew**.ða]

   ha-c**ia** ['a.s**ja**]

3. **I** and **u** next to each other can also form diphthongs. In this case, the SECOND one is the nucleus or the full vowel and the first one the semivowel or glide. They are always rising diphthongs:

   i + u: [s**ju**.'ðað] c**iu**-dad, ['b**ju**.ða] v**iu**-da

   u + i: [k**wi**.'ða.ðo] c**ui**-da-do, ['x**wi**-sjo] j**ui**-cio

Triphthongs

A **TRIPHTHONG** is a combination of a vocalic sound (glide **i** or **u**), a full vowel (**a**, **e**, **o**) and another vocalic sound (glide **i** or **u**) in the same syllable. Triphthongs are very rare and not typical for Spanish. The majority of triphthongs in the dictionary are either **ONOMATOPOEIA** (words that imitate the sound of a thing or an animal, for example **miau**), modern compound words (**semiautomático**, **biauricular**), and **INDIGENOUS WORDS** or **AMERICANISMS** (**aguaucle**, **guaicurú**). Furthermore, they can be found in Spain, in the second person plural of some verbs that end in –**iar** or –**uar**: **vosotros actuáis, amortiguáis, abreviáis, odiáis**, etc.

Hiatus

A **HIATUS** is a sequence of two full vowels that belong to two syllables: the open vowels [**a**], [**e**], [**o**] and the close stressed vowels [**i**], [**u**], written with an accent **í, ú**:

[a, e, o]:

['k**a**.**e**ɾ] c**a**-**e**r

[t**e**.'**a**-tɾo] t**e**-**a**-tro

['fe.**o**] fe-**o**

[**o**.'**e**s.te] **o**-**e**s-te

['k**a**.**o**s] c**a**-**o**s

[a, e, o] + [i, u]:

[r**a**.'**i**s] r**a**-**í**z

['g**i**.**a**] gu**í**-**a**

[r**e**.'**i**ɾ] r**e**-**í**r

[koɱ.'f**i**.**e**] con-f**í**-**e** (Subj. of 'confiar')

[**o**.'**i**.ðo] **o**-**í**-do

['l**i**.**o**] l**í**-**o**

[a.t**a**.'**u**ð] a-t**a**-**ú**d

['gɾ**u**.**a**] gr**ú**-**a**

[**re**.'**u**.no] **re-ú**-no (of reunir)

[ak.'**tu**.**e**] ac-**tú-e** (of actuar)

['d**u**.**o**] d**ú-o**

Knowing the difference between a full vowel, a diphthong, a triphthong and a hiatus is crucial for syllabification in Spanish (Chapter 3).

Questions

1. What is the difference between phonetics and phonemics/ phonology?
2. How are they related with orthography?
3. What are phonemes?
4. What is the International Phonetic Alphabet, and what is its purpose?
5. What do you know about the Spanish alphabet?
6. What is the difference between consonants and vowels?
7. How many consonants are there in Spanish?
8. What are full vowels, glides, diphthongs, and triphthongs? What is a hiatus?

Go further: Topics for presentations and discussions

1. The origins of writing; from orality to writing
2. The kinds of writing
3. The origins of Spanish
4. The evolution of Spanish orthography
5. Orthographic reforms of the Spanish language
6. Orthographical changes that were introduced in the *Ortografía de la RAE* in 2010
7. Orthographic ideals
8. The purpose of orthography
9. The origins and the evolution of the International Phonetic Alphabet (IPA)

Exercises

(If you do the exercises on-line, write all the words with upper case letters and use accents where they are necessary.)

1. **Fill the blanks with the terminology that was introduced in this chapter:**

Horizontal:

1 Sound that comes out of the mouth after going through an obstacle/ some kind of obstruction.

4 Sound that comes out of the mouth without any obstruction

6 Each of the graphic signs that constitute the alphabet of a language. (Another word for 'letter')

7 The combination of a vocalic sound (glide **i**, **u**), a full vowel (**a**, **e**, **o**) and another vocalic sound (glide **i**, **u**) in the same syllable.
10 The smallest and indivisible unit in the written language.
11 The little hump behind the upper teeth that can be felt easily with the tip of the tongue. (Two words; write it with _ in the middle when you do this exercise on-line.)
12 The combination of the nuclear vowels **a**, **e**, **o** with the unstressed high vowels **i** or **u**.
13 The sequence of two full vowels that belong to two syllables.

Vertical:

2 Another word for 'sound'.

3 Phonological unit able to distinguish different meanings.

5 Linguistic discipline that describes and regulates how a language is written.

8 Discipline that tries to establish families of sounds.

9 Discipline that studies all the sounds of a language and the acoustic differences that one can hear.

2. Find other comparisons to explain the concept of 'family of sounds'.

3. Indicate to which discipline the following definitions belong.

1= Orthography 2= Phonetics 3=Phonemics/Phonology

__ The root of this word comes from the Greek word "phonos", which means "sound" or "voice", and "ikos", which means "related to"

__ Science that deals with phonemes and their role in a language

__ The name comes from the Greek words "phonos" which means "sound" or "voice", and "logos", which means "study"

__ Discipline that deals with how a language is written

__ This discipline uses an ensemble of symbols, called "phonetic alphabet" to represent the sounds

__ Of Greek origin and means "correct writing"

__ Discipline that describes and explains the elements that make up the written form of the language

__ Discipline that deals with all the norms that regulate how a language is written

4. (D)iphthong, (T)riphthong or (H)iatus?

__ abstraído
__ aceite
__ actuáis
__ aéreo
__ aéreo
__ aire
__ aldea
__ ataúd
__ aullar
__ aurora
__ auto
__ boina
__ caer
__ canoa
__ causa
__ cloaca
__ coima
__ contagiéis
__ coreógrafa
__ creer
__ cuadra
__ cuento
__ deseo
__ día
__ ejecutéis
__ frío
__ fuego
__ gaucho
__ guardar
__ hacia
__ huaico
__ huay
__ huevo
__ incauto
__ jaula
__ jesuita
__ maestra
__ miau
__ miedo
__ monstruo
__ muelas
__ novia
__ oeste
__ oído
__ oigo
__ oír
__ país
__ paraguas
__ Paraguay
__ Paraguay
__ peinado
__ poeta
__ púa
__ raíz
__ reina
__ rueda
__ ruido

2

Spelling: problematic letters

Spanish is often called a phonetic language, implying that words are written the way they are pronounced, because in Spanish normally each sound is represented by just one letter or **DIGRAPH** (the combination of two simple letters, for example **ch**). For cultural and etymological reasons, however, there are some critical sounds that have a similar pronunciation but different spellings such as /x/, /k/, /b/, /β/ and /s/. The letter **h** is usually not pronounced. Since 1994, the digraphs **ch** and **ll** no longer officially have their own entry in the alphabet or in the dictionary and are integrated under the letters **c** and **l**. The same goes for **rr**, which never had a separate entry in the dictionary, even though it belongs to a different phoneme than **r**. This does not mean, however, that these digraphs have disappeared from the Spanish writing system.

The Spanish Language Academies also recommend using just one name for each letter or digraph of the Spanish alphabet. (Traditionally people used several names for some letters.)

Figure 1. Sign with non-standard spelling: "Se nesecita mosa(o)" instead of "Se necesita moza(o)"

Students who learn Spanish as a second language usually use vocabulary lists to memorize new words. Therefore, they normally know how to write the words that could cause problems before they know how they are pronounced. Spanish speaking children usually learn to speak first. They start writing and learn how to write later, for example in school, when they also start reading. People who do not read or who have not had a formal education often use non-standardized spelling when it comes to writing something, as can be seen in the sign on the previous page.

Even in Spanish, not everything is written the way it is pronounced, and sometimes only the dictionary can clarify the correct spelling.

Foreign language students and people who know many languages have the advantage that they may know how a word is written in the language where it originated, for example in Latin or Greek. English also has incorporated many words from these two languages, directly or indirectly, just like Spanish. Therefore, spelling in English or other languages may sometimes help to predict the correct spelling in Spanish.

The sound [x]

This sound can be written with the letters **j**, **g** and occasionally with the letter **x**.

It is always written **j** before **a**, **o**, **u** and at the end of words: **jamón, jorobado, jubilar, escojo, dejan, reloj.**

Before **e** and **i**, however, it is written

1. j: **jinete, jerarquía, alebrije**, etc.
2. g: **gemir, ginebra, escoger,** etc.
3. **x** (occasionally): **México, Oaxaca, Xavier**, etc.

If, for whatever reason, you do not have access to a dictionary, you can try to make an educated guess whether a word is written with **g** or **j**. Does the same word with the same meaning exist in English? If this is the case and the English word is written with a **j**, the word in Spanish is also written with **j**: **adjetivo** (Engl. adjective), **majestad** (Engl. majesty), **subjetivo** (Engl. subjective), **sujeto** (Engl. subject), **objetivo** (Engl. objective), etc. If it starts with a **g** in English, it is very likely that it is also written with a **g** in Spanish: **género** (Engl. gender), **génesis** (Engl. génesis), **gigante** (Engl. giant), **general** (Engl. general), etc. This is because English has kept the etymological **g**. (The word **jirafa** <del it. *giraffa*; engl. giraffe> is an exception.) There are some more of these practical rules that generally work fairly well, even though there are no rules without exceptions.

■ The letter j

Words in which the sound [x] before /e/ and /i/ almost exclusively is written **j** are:

1. Words that start with **eje-** in Spanish. In English, they are written with **x** which is pronounced [ks]: **eje** (Engl. `axis`), **ejecutar** (Engl. `to execute`), **ejecutivo** (Engl. `executive`), **ejemplo** (Engl. `example`), **ejercer** (Engl. `to exercise`), **ejercicio** (Engl. `exercise`), **ejecutar** (Engl. `to execute`).

2. Words that end in **-aje** (many of them are loan words from French) and **-eje**: **abordaje**, **coraje**, **dopaje**, **encaje**, **garaje**, **hospedaje**, **lenguaje**, **mensaje**, **paisaje**, **salvaje**, **despeje**, **hereje**, etc.

3. Words that end in **-jero**: **cajero**, **callejero**, **consejero**, **extranjero**, **pasajero**, **viajero**, etc. (The word **ligero** is not an exception because here **-jero** is not a suffix, but part of a primary word <Fr. `léger`>).

4. When a word is derived from a primary word that is written with **–j**, **-jo** or **–ja**, the **j** is maintained: **consejero** < **consejo**, **enrojecer** < **rojo**, **fijeza** < **fijo**, **granjero** < **granja**, **hojear** < **hoja**, **espejeo** < **espejo**, **vejez** < **viejo**, etc.

■ The letter g

1. As mentioned before, there are many words that Spanish inherited from Latin, Greek, French, Italian and other languages that start with **gene-**, **geni-**, **geno-**, **genu-**: **generoso**, **género**, **genético**, **genio**, **genital**, **genocidio**, **genoma**, **genuino**, etc.

2. The same goes for Greco-Latin roots or elements or learned words, for example:

   a. geo-: **geógrafo**, **geometría**, **geopolítico**, etc.

   b. **german(o)-**: **germanista**, **germánico**, etc.

c. **ger(onto)-**: **geriatría**, **gerontólogo**, etc.

d. **gine(co)-**: **ginecólogo**, **ginefobia**, etc.

e. **legi-**: **legible**, **legión**, **legítimo**, etc.

Exceptions are the words derived from **lejos** which is a very common word that comes from Latin `laxius`.)

f. Words ending in **-gésimo**: **vigésimo**, etc.

g. Words ending in **-ginoso/a**: **vertiginoso**, etc.

h. Words ending in **-logía**: **ecología**, **filosofía**, etc.

3. Words that contain **-inge-**: **ingeniero**, **faringe**, **ingerir** ('to put something in the mouth, especially food and drinks') etc. *EXCEPTION: Another word with similar meaning, **injerir** ('to insert one thing in another') and its derivatives are written with **j**: **injerencia**, **injerta**, **injertable**, **injertar**, etc.

4. Many words with **-gen-**: **aborigen**, **argentino**, **gente**, etc., BUT there are exceptions, for example the derivatives of words written with **j** (see the letter **j**), among others.

5. Words with **gest-**: **congestión**, **gesto**, **sugestionable**, etc. (BUT: **majestad** and its derivatives and **vejestorio**).

6. Words containing **-gia** or **-gio** (also **-gía** and **-gío**): **analogía**, **cirugía**, **demagogia**, etc. (BUT there are several exceptions, for example **herejía**)

7. The infinitives of the verbs in **-ger**, **-gir**: **coger**, **proteger**, **surgir**, etc. (EXCEPTIONS ARE: **tejer** and its derivatives and **crujir**.) In the verb conjugations, of course, there can be a **j**: **yo protejo**, **quiero que surja**, etc.

■ The letter x

Until the beginning of the nineteenth century, the sound [x] could also be written **x**. In 1815, the Royal Spanish Language Academy decided to eliminate the use of the grapheme **x** for this sound. Nevertheless, this spelling has been conserved in some names of places or proper names, for example **México** and **Oaxaca**.

There are those –of course no Mexicans– that want to write **México** with a **j** instead of **x**. Just find a Mexican stamp, coin, or bill to see how the name of the country is really written.

The sounds [g] and [ɣ]

This sound, for example in **gato**, is written **gu-** before **-e** or **-i**: **guerra**, **guiar** and only **g-** before **–a**, **-o**, and **–u**: **ganar**, **gol**, **gusano**. If there are two dots on top of the **u** (ü) –that are also called diaeresis– before an **-e** or **-i**, the **u** sounds like [w]. Examples are **bilingüe**, **argüir**, **lingüística**, etc.

Often we have to add an **u** to conserve the [**g**] sound in some conjugated forms of **-ar** verbs: **agregar** → **agregué**; **alargar** → **alargue**; **colgar** → **cuelgue**; **entregar** → **entregué**; **pegar** → **pegué**, etc.

The sounds [b] and [β]

The letters **b** and **v** are pronounced the same way in the same phonetic context, [b] at the beginning of a word or after silence and after a nasal sound (**boca**, **vocal**, **bomba**); [**β**] in all other contexts (**nueve**, **cabe**, **calvo**), similar to the pronunciation of the **w** in `wagon`. Often, the comparison with English or other languages helps because there are many **COGNATES** that use the same consonant. Other words, if you do not know them yet, you will have to memorize: cognates with **b**: **bisonte**, **búlgaro**, **Bulgaria**, **bronquitis**, **Bolivia**, etc.; cognates with **v**: **visión**, **vulgar**, **vocabulario**, etc.

The sound [k]

The letters c and qu

The sound [k] is mostly written **c** before **a**, **o**, **u**, and consonant, as well as at the end of some **ONOMATOPOEIA** or word taken from other languages. It is written **qu** before **e** and **i**:

- **c + a, o, u: casa**, **columna**, **cuñado**, **pescar**, **poco**, **escuchar**, **delincuente** etc.
- c + **consonant**: **claro**, **pacto**, **técnico**, etc.
- **c** at the end: **clic**, **crac**, **tictac**, etc.
- **qu + e, i**: **queso**, **química**, **enloquecer**, etc.

The **u** after **q**- followed by **e** or **i** is never pronounced: **que**, **quizá**. The **u** after **c** followed by **a**, **e**, **i** or **o** sounds like [w]: **cuánto**, **cuento**, **cuidado**, **cuota**.

The letter k

In a few foreign words, the sound [k] is written **k**: **bikini**, **kilómetro**, **Kremlin**, **vikingo**, **kiosko**, **vodka**, **paprika**, **euskera**, **kimono**, **kaki**, **kipá**, **kiwi**, **koala**, etc. However, there are variants of some of them that follow the more typical writing with **qu**: **biquini**, **quiosco**, **caqui**, etc.

The sound [ɟ]

Today, most Spanish speakers do not distinguish the pronunciation of the phonemes /ɟ/ (written **y**) and /ʎ/ (written **ll**). This reality is often called **YEÍSMO**. A yeísta speaker does not distinguish the pronunciation of the words **vaya** (form of **ir**) and **valla** (Engl. `fence`). Both are pronounced ['ba.ʝa]. Therefore, it is sometimes difficult to know if a word is written with **y** or with **ll**.

To illustrate this phenomenon, we would like to quote a little paragraph from a collection of short stories by the Spanish writer Almudena Grandes, called "Modelos de mujer". In it, a girl that lives with her family in Madrid talks about the characteristic Castilian spoken in the rural regions of Burgos and Segovia of her nanny Piedad:

> [Ella] "distinguía perfectamente entre la pronunciación de **poyo*** y la de **pollo**, y bromeaba afirmando que en mi casa, todos los jueves,

se comía banco de piedra estofado". (1996, 212) ([She] perfectly distinguished the pronunciation of **poyo*** and **pollo**, and had fun saying that in my house, every Thursday, we ate stuffed stone bench."

*(*Poyo = Bench made of stone or other material, attached to the wall)*

If you don't know how the sound is spelled, you will have to look the word up in the dictionary.

The **y** represents the sound in the conjugation: **cayeron** (of **caer**), **leyendo** (of **leer**), **oyó** (of **oír**), **hayan** (of **haber**), **yendo** (of **ir**); and in other word forms that stem from those verbs: **concluyente**, **contribuyente**, **oyente**, etc.

The sound [s]

Today, most Spanish speakers (and all Spanish speakers living in America, the Canary Islands and most people living in Andalusia) do not distinguish the pronunciation of the letters **s**, **z** and **c** (before **e** and **i**). This reality is called **SESEO** and has caused a lot of confusion, especially among people that do not write often.

The sound [s], for example in the English word `sing`, can be written in 4 different ways in Spanish: **s**, **c**, **z**, and **x**.

The letter **s** is pronounced like the basic [s] in English before any vowel. In Latin America, the **c** + **e** or **i** and the **z** before any vowel are also pronounced [s].

The letter **z** in Spanish is never pronounced as a voiced [z], such as in the English word `zebra`, unless it comes before a voiced consonant. (See Chapter 9)

At the beginning of words that stem from Greek, for example **xenofobia**, **xerocopia**, **xilófono**, etc., and in relaxed speech before consonant, the **x** can also be pronounced [s], for example **extra** (= [ˈ**es**.tra]).

The letter h

Even though the **h** is generally not pronounced, which means that it is not aspirated as in English, it has survived in Spanish for etymological and historical reasons. We say that it is silent.

Most cases of **h** come from Classical Latin, where the **h** originally represented an aspirated sound, which, together with its graphic representation, had already disappeared at the beginning of the Imperial period. Therefore, we can find in the first medieval texts spellings such as omne (today **hombre**) and onor (today **honor**). However, since the beginning of the 13th century and especially in the 15th century, a renaissance of Latin caused the re-introduction of the etymological **h** in writing, and as a result, we must write it today even though it is silent.

Another origin of **h** in Spanish is an **f** at the beginning of Latin words (**harina**, from Lat. farīna). The letter **h** originated also in loan words from other languages, for example Arabic: **alcohol**, **hasta**; French: **higiene**, **hotel**; English: **hamburguesa**, **hipnotismo**; and others.

Finally, there are cases that cannot be explained with etymological reasons, for example the switch from **o** to **hue** in the conjugation of the verb **oler** < **huele**.

If you don't know if a word is written with or without an **h**, if you don't know its etymology, and if you cannot find cognates in English or other languages, you must use a dictionary. The following are some general rules:

Use an **h** in the following cases:

1. Before the diphthongs /ua/, /ue/, /ui/, at the beginning of words or stressed syllables within words: **hueco**, **huella**, **huelga**, **huir**, **huele**, **cacahuete**, etc.

2. Before the diphthongs /ia/, /ie/ at the beginning of words: **hiato**, **hielo**, **hierba**, **hierro**, etc.

Questions

1. People say that Spanish is a 'phonetic language'. What does this mean? Is this correct?
2. What is the advantage of knowing other languages for knowing how certain words are written in Spanish? Does this advantage apply to spelling all Spanish words?
3. What is the difference between letters, sounds and families of sounds? How are they written in this book?
4. How is the sound [x] written in Spanish? If you don't have a dictionary, how can you guess the spelling of this sound? Give some examples from this book and find others in the dictionary.
5. How are the sounds [b] and [β] written in Spanish? If you don't have a dictionary, how can you guess the spelling of this sound? Give some examples from this book and find others in the dictionary.
6. How is the sound [k] written in Spanish? If you don't have a dictionary, how can you guess the spelling of this sound? Give some examples from this book and find others in the dictionary.
7. How is the sound [s] written in Spanish? If you don't have a dictionary, how can you guess the spelling of this sound? Give some examples from this book and find others in the dictionary.
8. How is the sound [ʝ] written in Spanish? Are the different spellings pronounced the same way in the entire Spanish speaking world? If you don't have a dictionary, how can you guess the spelling of this sound? Give some examples from this book and find others in the dictionary.
9. Is the letter **h** pronounced in Spanish? How can you guess if a word is written with or without an **h**?

Go further: Topics for presentations and discussions

1. Compare the alphabet of the Royal Spanish Language Academy (RAE) with the following alphabet:

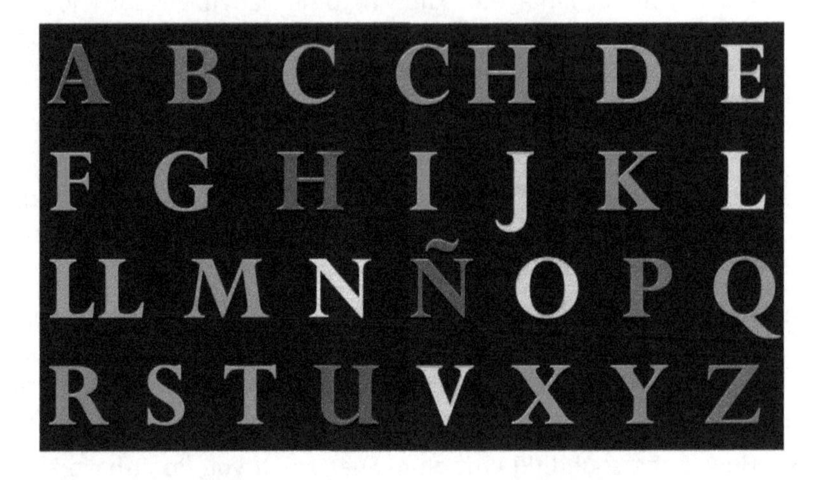

   How do they differ? You can find the answer in the following RAE Web page: https://www.rae.es/recursos/ortografia/ ortografia -2010.

2. Ask someone whose native language is English to spell the words `occurred`, `separate`, `license`, `plagiarism` and other words that might be used in 'spelling bee' competitions. Then do the same with Spanish native speaker and ask them to spell the following words: **equivocarse, bacanal, consanguinidad, convalecencia, dislexia, expectativa, hemiplejía, infligido, hurgar**, etc. Do they spell the same way in both languages? If they don't, what may be the reasons?

Exercises

1. **Fill in the spaces with the correct letter that represents the [x] sound. In the cases where the English equivalent is similar to the Spanish word, compare the two spellings. Spell the Spanish words the way Spanish speakers would do.**

el ___apón
___enerar dinero
___enético
___eométrico
el espiona___e
___erusalén
___oven
el ___enitivo
___udicial
aconse___ar
ad___etivo
ba___arse del carro
el cora___e
de___ar de hablar
yo de__é de __ugar
el porcenta___e
el ___ardín
el ___emelo
el ___énero
el ___énesis
el ___igante
el ___udaísmo
el ___ueves
el aprendiza___e

el gara___e
el lengua___e
la mon___a
el pasa___e
empu__ar
en __eneral
la __ente
la __itana
la __oya
la __ungla
la __usticia
la venta__a
Mé__ico
aconse__ar
¡Aconsé__eme!
salva__e
e__emplo
el in__eniero
Oa__aca
el e__ercicio
el ___erente
el cora__e
ro__o
el via__ero

2. **Fill in the spaces with the correct letter that represents the [g] sound. Spell the Spanish words the way Spanish speakers would do.**

- La __allina pone huevos, el ___allo no.
- La Se___unda ___erra Mundial terminó en 1945.
- El entre___a su informe sobre ___oya.
- La ___errilla Sendero Luminoso existió en Perú.
- La ___inea Ecuatorial es un país en África.
- La ___arantía caduca en un mes.
- El meren___e es un baile típico de la República Dominicana.
- Me duele la ___ar___anta.
- En Europa hay muchos alber___es juveniles.
- La ___itarra es un instrumento de música.

3. **Fill in the spaces with the correct letter(s) that represent(s) the [k] sound. Spell the Spanish words the way Spanish speakers would do.**

el ___ilo
ad___irir
a___ello
ar___eológi___o
al___ilar
el ata___e
blan___o
a___í
el ___eso
el blo___e
___alifi___ar

es___iar
el bos___e
la es___ina
el ___ilómetro
el ___ími___o
la ta___illa
el papri___a
___ebrar
el ___as___o
tran___ilo
me___áni___o

in___ai___o
vol___áni__o
el __iosco
enlo__ecer
eus__era
el bi_ini
cin_o
sa_ar
yo sa_qué
coloca_ar
yo colo_é

4. **Fill in the spaces with the correct letter that represents the [s] sound. Spell the Spanish words the way Spanish speakers would do.**

   - ¿Vamos ___in o con Juan?
   - ¿Es ___imple o difí___il?
   - Yo soy un hombre ___in___ero, de donde cre__e la palma.
   - ¿Quién no cono__e La ___infonía número 9 de Beethoven?
   - Treinta y __inco (35) y veinti__inco (25) son ___e___enta (60).
   - La ___e___e___ión o separación definitiva de Portugal de España ocurre en 1640.
   - Contemos: ___ero, uno, do___, tre___, cuatro, ___inco, ___eis, ___iete, die___, on___e, do___e, tre___e, cator___e, quin___e, die___iseis, ...
   - ¡Luchemos por la pa___ en el mundo!
   - Los Amish son pa___ifistas.
   - La capital de Vene___uela es Caraca___.
   - El oxígeno es un ga___.
   - La capa___idad de esta sala es ___incuenta per___onas
   - Vivimos en el segundo pi___o de la ca___a.
   - Tienes que ven___er la pere___a si quieres sacar buenas nota___.
   - Sui___a y Sue___ia son dos paí__es europeos.

5. **Is there an h in the following words?**

   - Este muchacho es capaz de ___acer el trabajo porque es muy ___ábil.
   - El pobre niño es ___uérfano.
   - El ___acero es un metal.
   - John ___abla español.
   - Mira ___acia la derecha.

- Una ___acacia es un árbol o ___arbusto de flores ___olorosas.
- El pan se hace con ___arina y ___agua.
- Giuliani fue un ___alcalde muy conocido de Nueva York.
- Ya no puedo más. Estoy ___arto de tus ___istorias.
- Un ___istmo es una lengua de tierra que une dos continentes o una península con un continente.
- ___ay un ___ueco en la blusa.
- Las gallinas ponen ___uevos.
- El perfume ___uele muy bien.
- No quiero ___oler su perfume.
- Hay muchos ___indúes en la India.
- ¿Qué ___ora es a___ora?
- ¡___ojalá venga Juan!

6. **Write the Spanish equivalents of the following English words. They are very similar.**

Horizontal:

1 courage; 6 garage; 7 kilo, 10 exercise; 12 percentage; 13 executive; 14 passenger

Vertical:

2 giraffe; 3 savage; 4 secession; 5 chemical; 6 genesis; 8 language; 9 hierarchy; 11 example

7. **Dictation: Write what you hear.**

3

Syllabification in Spanish

Word-processing programs work beautifully for dividing syllables and putting hyphens in the right place. If it's all so automatic, why should you learn how to do it manually?

One answer is because this is a book about phonetics and phonemics and dividing words at the end of a line is part of orthography, which represents sounds in writing. As we have stated earlier, the spelling of a word is determined in large part by how it is pronounced. That is why phonetic syllables, considered the smallest prosodic or rhythmic units, are not very different from written syllables. However, there are some differences and several specific rules in standard orthography. Let's take the following sentence as an example: ***Las águilas imperiales en el aire buscan otra presa.*** There are 44 letters, 8 spaces and 9 words. The places where the sentence can be hyphenated are: **Las águi-las im-pe-ria-les en el ai-re bus-can otra pre-sa.**

Even though there are three phonetic syllables in **á-gui-las** and two in **o-tra**, these words cannot be hyphenated after the first syllable, because, according to the *Ortografía de la lengua española*, "when the first syllable of a word consists just of one vowel, a hyphen should be placed after it at the end of a line to prevent this vowel from standing alone at the end of the line: **abo-/ lengo**, and not ***a-bolengo** ..." (2010, 406)

The spoken form of this sentence can be transcribed as follows (The dots divide the syllables):

[la.ˈsa.ɣi.la.sim.pe.ˈrja.le.se.ne.ˈlaj.re | ˈbus.ka.ˈno.tra.ˈpre.sa]

When you read the sentence correctly, you can hear only two phonological phrases that are divided by a little break (represented by the vertical bar **|**). You can also see that there are 18 syllables instead of 16 in writing and that the limits of the syllables are different, because in spoken Spanish, whenever possible, a syllable should end with a vowel. Such a syllable is called an **OPEN SYLLABLE**. To achieve this, we connect consonants and vowels whenever there is a consonant at the end of a word and a vowel at the beginning of the next word. Therefore, knowing the syllabification, also helps to link words, emphasize vowels, and produce the typical rhythm and sound of Spanish.

Another example is the letter **x** in **taxi**. At the end of the line in writing, this word is divided **ta-xi**. Phonetically, however, it is divided [ˈtak.si] because in this position, the letter **x** is pronounced with two sounds, [k] + [s].

Still another example is the morphological division. Compound words that exist as independent words as well as productive prefixes + independent words can be divided phonetically or morphologically at the end of a line. Examples are: **bie-nes-tar** or **bien-es-tar**, **reins-ta-lar** or **re-ins-ta-lar**. (You can find more examples in the *Ortografía de la lengua española*, §4.1.1.1.1.2.)

Knowing how to divide words and phrases phonetically and how many syllables there are also helps to determine where the stress (**ACENTO PROSÓDICO** or **ACENTO DE INTENSIDAD**) is and whether or not it is necessary to add a written accent, that is also called **TILDE**.

In this chapter we will explain the syllabification rules for words and in Chapter 14 for larger unit, such as phrases, clauses, sentences, and phonological phrases.

What is a syllable?

A syllable in phonetics is the smallest rhythmic unit. Each syllable consists of one or several sounds.

A syllable has, at minimum, a **NUCLEUS** (Span. **NÚCLEO**), which is always a vowel and that always stands out in speech. A word has as many syllables as nuclear vowels. This vowel can be accompanied by one or two additional vowel sounds that are called **GLIDES** (Span. **DESLIZADAS**). Together they form **DIPHTHONGS** (Span. **DIPTONGOS**) and **TRIPHTHONGS** (Span. **TRIPTONGOS**). The vowel can also be preceded or followed by one or several consonants. The part before the nucleus is called the **ONSET** (Span. **ATAQUE**), and the sounds that can follow are called the **CODA**. The nucleus and the coda together make up the **RHYME** (Span. **RIMA**).

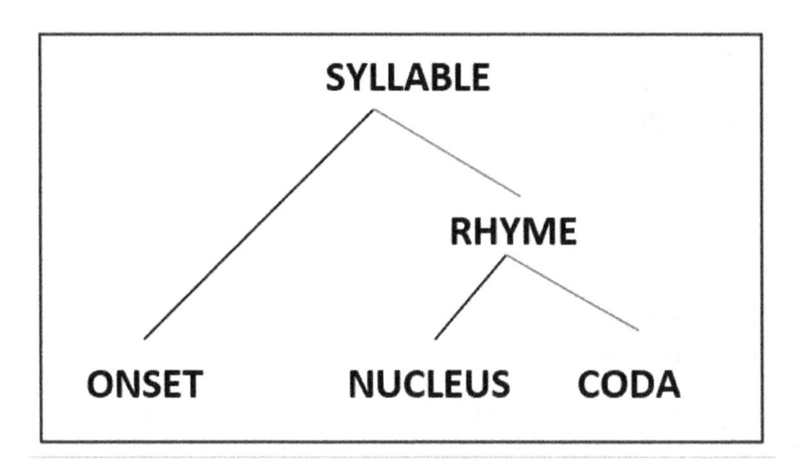

1 vowel:

['**a**.xo] (**a-jo**, Engl. `garlic`)

1 vowel + 1 or 2 glides:

['**we**.le] (**hue-le**, Inf. of **oler**), ['**aj**.re] (**ai-re**), ['b**jej**.ra] (**viei-ra**, Engl. `scallop`)

1 vowel (+ 1 or 2 glides) + up to 3 consonants:

['**pa**.xa] (**pa-ja**, Engl. `straw`); ['**pwe.**ðe] (**pue-de**); [**plu**.'ral] (**plu-ral**) [**kons-truk**-'sjon] (**cons-truc-ción**)

■ How are words divided into syllables in Spanish?

Other than in English, where it is sometimes not so easy to decide where to divide a word, the rules in Spanish are very clear and unambiguous. Here are the three rules that you must know:

Rule #1: ...V.CV.C... [o.'re.xa] (o-re-ja)

When vowels and consonants alternate, syllables are divided AFTER the vowel. The consonant starts the next syllable:

[fo.'ne.ti.ka] (fo-né-ti-ca)
['nu.me.ro] (nú-me-ro)
[re.no.'βa.ða] (re-no-va-da)
['ko.me] (co-me)
['ka.ɟe] (ca-lle)
['ko.tʃe] (co-che)
['ko.re] (co-rre)
['ka.ɲa] (ca-ña)
[ko.mu.ni.'ka.ðo] (co-mu-ni-ca-do)

As you can see, all the syllables in the previous examples are open syllables. This means that they end in vowels. This type of syllable is the most frequent in Spanish.

The letter **x** requires some additional remarks because depending on its positions in the word and the preferences of the speakers, it can be pronounced differently, just as one sound or as two sounds. It can be pronounced **[x]** in the word **México**, such as in **mejor**; **[s]** at the beginning of words, for example in **xenophobia**, such as in **semáforo**; **[ks]** or **[gs]** in intervocalic position, before another consonant or at the end of words, for example in the words **exhibir**, **extra** or **taxi**. In informal or relaxed speech, it can also be pronounced [s] before a consonant, for example in **extra**, which sounds like **['es.tra]**. For the purpose of orthographic hyphenation at the end of a line, the **x** is always considered a consonant. In the phonetic transcription, on the other hand, it can represent various sounds: **['tak.si]**.

If there are two or three vowel sounds between consonants, we are dealing either with a **HIATUS**, a **DIPHTHONG** or a **TRIPHTHONG**.

HIATUS: Two mid/ low vowels **[a, e, o]** cannot be part of the same syllable. They are divided among two syllables: ['k**a.e**] (ca-e, 3rd person present of **caer**), ['kr**e.e**] (cre-e, 3rd person present of **creer**), etc.

HIATUS: A mid or low vowel and a stressed high vowel (with a written accent) cannot be part of the same syllable either: ['fr**i.o**] (frí-o), ['d**u.o**] (dú-o), etc.

According to the Royal Spanish Language Academy, an **h** between two vowels is not considered a consonant because it is silent, and therefore in the conjugation of the verb **prohibir** a written accent on the **i** is required to prevent a diphthong: [pro.'i.βe] (pro-hí-be). The same goes for the words **ahínco** (`effort`), **mohíno** (`mournful`), **búho** (`owl`) and **ahíto** (`tired of`).

DIPHTHONG: The combination of a mid or low and an unstressed high vowel is not divided into different syllables: ['**aw**.to] (au-to), ['**we**.le] (hue-le). etc.

Combinations with an **h** between the vowels also form diphthongs: [**aj**.'ɟa.ðo] (ahi-ja-do), [**aw**.'ma.ðo] (ahu-ma-do), [de.s**aw**.'sjar] (de-sahu-ciar, Engl. `cancel`, `terminate`) and the related words **desahucio** and **desahuciadamente**.

TRIPHTHONG: The sequence of unstressed high vowel + mid or low vowel (nucleus) + unstressed high vowel is NOT divided into different syllables: [b**jaw**.ri.ku.'lar] (biau-ri-cu-lar).

There is a triphthong in the name **Uruguay** [u.ru.g**waj**], but not in the adjective **uruguayo** [u.ru.'g**wa**.ɟo]. The letter **y** here represents the consonant [ɟ].

Rule #2.1: ...V.CC.V... [de.'tras] (de-trás) with CLUSTER

If there are TWO consonants between vowels,
and they are a combination of **p, t, c, b, d, g, f** + **l** or **r**,
they represent a **CLUSTER**
and are NOT divided.
The syllable is divided BEFORE the cluster:

['ko.**pla**] (co-pla)
['a.**bla**] (ha-bla)
['o.**bra**] (o-bra)

The general rule is that if a group of sounds can start a word, it can also start a syllable, and in Spanish there are many words that start with the combination of **p, t, c, b, d, g, f** + **l** or **r**, for example **placer**, **tres**, **clase**, **creer**, **blando**, **brillo**, **drama**, **grillo**, **global**, **frente**, **flaco**, etc.

Rule #2.2: ...V.CC.V... ['kam.po] (cam-po)

Any other combination of two (2) consonants
is divided in the middle:

['al.ɣo] (al-go)
[ak.'sjon] (ac-ción)
[es.'tar] (es-tar)
[in.'sis.te] (in-sis-te)
[kol.'tʃon] (col-chón)
['siŋ.ko] (cinco)
['san̪.t̪a] (san-ta)

Be careful with the combination **s** + consonant, especially **st** and **sp**, because unlike in English, both letters ARE DIVIDED in Spanish: (Engl.) `per-spec-tive` but (Span.) **pers-pec-ti-va**, (Engl.) `con-sti-tu-tion` but (Span.) **cons-ti-tu-ción**. The reason for this is the same rule that we mentioned before. Just ask yourself if there are words in Spanish that start with **st** and **sp**. The answer, of course, is NO. There are no words in Spanish that start with **s** + consonant, for example **st-**, **sp-**, **sc-**, etc. (`star` = **estrella**, `ski` = **esquí**). Therefore, combinations of **s** + consonant are divided after the **s**.

Rule #3.1: ...VCCCV.../...VCCCV ... [kum.'plir] (cum-plir)

If there are THREE (3) or FOUR (4) consonants together
and one of them IS NOT an **s**,
we always divide AFTER the first consonant
because the second and third must be CLUSTER
with the letters **p**, **t**, **c**, **b**, **d**, **g**, **f** + **l** or **r** that are NOT divided:

[koɱ.flu.'ʝen.te] (con-flu-yen-te)

[mal.'krja.ðo] (mal-cria-do)

[kom.'prar] (com-prar)

['kon̪.t̪ra] (con-tra)

Rule #3.2: ...VCCCV.../...VCCCV ...
['mons.trwo] (mons-truo)

If there are THREE (3) or FOUR (4) consonants together
and one of them IS an **s**,
we always divide AFTER the **s**:

[ins.'tan.te] (ins-tan-te)

[kons.truk.'sjon] (cons-truc-ción)

[abs.'trak.to] (abs-trac-to)

If there is ever a doubt as to where to break syllables in a word with two or more consonants between vowels, here is a sure-fire alternate system: Look at the combination of consonants after the vowel. If they can start a word, then the syllable breaks right after the vowel. If the remaining consonant or consonants can start a word, you have found the beginning of the next syllable, if not, continue adding consonants to the previous syllable until the remaining consonant or group of consonants can start a word.

Example 1: **CONTRASTE**

NTR: No, a word cannot start with NTR-.

TR: Yes, a word can start with TR-.

The first syllable is *CON-*.

ST: No, a word cannot start with ST-.

T: Yes, a word can start with T-.

The second syllable is *-TRAS-* and the third syllable is *-TE*

Ejemplo 2: **SOLSTICIO**

LST: No, a word cannot start with LST-.

ST: No, a word cannot start with ST-.

T: Yes, a word can start with T-.

The first syllable is *SOLS-*. The second syllable is *-TI- and* the third is *-CIO*.

Questions

1. What is a syllable? Are written and spoken syllables identical?
2. What is an open syllable, and what is its role in Spanish?
3. What are the particularities of the graphemes **ch**, **ll**, **ñ** and **rr**?
4. What are the particularities of the letter **x**?
5. What does "morphological hyphenation" mean?
6. What does every syllable have?
7. What else can be part of a syllable?
8. What are the different parts of a syllable called?
9. Can there be more than one vowel in a syllable?
10. What are glides? Give examples.
11. What are diphthongs? Give examples.
12. Is there a diphthong in the word **ahumado**?
13. Why do we have to write **yo prohíbo** with a written accent on the **i**?
14. What are triphthongs? Give examples.
15. Is there a triphthong in the word **Uruguay**? Why or why not?
16. Is there a triphthong in the word **uruguayo**? Why or why not?
17. What is a hiatus? Give examples.
18. How is the sequence ... **VCVC** ... divided?
19. How is the sequence ... **VCCV** ... divided?
20. How are the sequences ... **VCCCV** ... and ... **VCCCCV** ... divided?

Exercises

1. (D)iphthong, (T)riphthong or (H)iatus?

- ☐ Paraguay
- ☐ uruguayo
- ☐ ahuecar
- ☐ caída
- ☐ huelga
- ☐ anchoa
- ☐ loable
- ☐ prohíbe
- ☐ vehículo
- ☐ búho
- ☐ cacahuate
- ☐ recio
- ☐ antiguo
- ☐ deuda
- ☐ veinte
- ☐ tenue
- ☐ viuda
- ☐ juez
- ☐ teatro
- ☐ feo
- ☐ caos
- ☐ raíz
- ☐ oído
- ☐ grúa
- ☐ dúo
- ☐ héroe
- ☐ poeta

2. Break the following words into syllables.

abstenerse
aéreo
afear
albedrío
anchoa
apeo
apio
Babieca
balneario
beodo
bisiesto
boxeo
caer
calle
cambio
Casildea
circunstancia
coexiste
coincide
cojeo
constaba
Constanza
constelaciones
consternar
constitucional
constituida
construcción
construido
construir
críe
dalia
deificar
deleite
delirio
derrocar
descuidado
deseo
deshacer
deuda
egoísmo
empeora
enfrío
envío
estadounidense
exacto
examen
fíen

fraseología	legible	ruido
heroína	llenar	ruin
hinchar	loable	soez
inconstante	magia	sois
intersticio	malcriado	solsticio
instala	monstruo	sonreirá
instante	oboe	superstición
instar	paranoia	teísmo
instilar	poema	trascendental
instinto	reconstitución	transductor
institución	reinstalar	triunfa
instructor	remedio	tuición
instrumento	residuo	veintiuno
jaez	retroactivo	vídeo

3. Break the following words into syllables.

ampliación	ejemplificación
ampliamente	implacable
autoempleo	influyente
complaciente	instruido
complejidad	monstruosamente
construcción	obstruccionismo
contemplativo	reconstrucción
desobstrucción	substrato
desprestigio	desproporcional

4
Stress: When is a written accent necessary?

Words are the smallest independent units of meaning. Their pronunciation, meaning and use is described in the dictionary. In Spanish, with a few exceptions, each word has only one stressed syllable. What distinguishes stressed syllables from unstressed syllables phonetically is a stronger articulatory effort, which manifests itself in a higher pitch, the expelling of more air and a small increase in length and intensity. All the other syllables are unstressed. The only exception are adverbs ending in -**mente**, which have two (2) stressed syllables because they maintain the original stressed syllable of the adjective while adding a second stressed syllable in **-mente**, which comes from the Latin noun `mens, mentis`: **ágilmente**, **altamente**, etc.

Stress is used to distinguish words with different meanings, for example **libro** vs. **libró**, **célebre** vs. **celebré**.

When words are used in larger utterances, e.g. phrases or sentences, not all the words are stressed. This will be explained further in Chapter 14.

Most words in Spanish have the stress on the second to last syllable. They are called **LLANAS** in Spanish. They are followed in frequency by words that have the stress on the last syllable, called **AGUDAS** in Spanish. Finally, there are some words that have the stress on the antepenult (third syllable from the last). Many of them are scholarly words, loan words from Latin, classical Greek, and other languages, for example Italian, French, English, and indigenous languages. These words are called **ESDRÚJULAS** in Spanish. There are even a few words that have the stress on the fourth syllable from the last, called **SOBRESDRÚJULAS**. In general, these are word forms consisting of an imperative or a gerund and one or several pronouns at the end, for example **repítemelo**.

We must distinguish the **STRESS** (Span. **ACENTO PROSÓDICO**) that can be heard when people are speaking from the written accent, that is also called **TILDE** (´) in Spanish. We only use a written accent to indicate that there is an exception from the two prototypical rules of pronunciation.

In order to know if a word is written with or without a written accent, it is necessary to know how words are divided into syllables and what is a **DIPHTHONG**, a **TRIPHTHONG** or a **HIATUS**.

Llanas

Due to the evolution of Spanish, most words have the stress on the SECOND TO LAST (PENULTIMATE) syllable. These words are called **LLANAS** or also **GRAVES**.

Llanas and the written accent (TILDE):

1. Words ending in a vowel, **–s** or **–n**, are written WITHOUT a written accent on the nuclear vowel of the stressed syllable.

hablo	**origen**	**continuos**	**ojo**
habla	**crimen**	**tribu**	**ojos**
hablas	**examen**	**tribus**	**taxi**
hablan	**continuo**	**dosis**	**taxis**

   Examples with diphthongs and hiatus are: **aduana**, **acuerdo**, **chequeo**, **idea**, **pelea**, **prohíbe**, etc.

2. LLANAS that end in a consonant other than **–s** or **–n** must be written with a TILDE on the nuclear vowel of the stressed syllable.

difícil	**árbol**	**almíbar**	**Martínez**
tórax	**mármol**	**fácil**	**cráter**
lápiz	**carácter**	**sándwich**	**dólar**

3. There must be a written accent on words that end with a HIATUS containing **/i/** or **/u/**, for example **mayoría**, **grúa**, **tía**, **acentúa**, **sería**, **hacía**, **continúo** etc., because the stress is on the **i** and the **u** of the second to last syllable. However, the use of the written accent in this context is not really an exception from the rules of pronunciation of LLANAS. The tilde only shows that we are dealing

with a HIATUS and not with a DIPHTHONG. Even an **h** between the two vowels doesn't prevent a DIPHTHONG from forming in words like **prohíbe** or **búho** if we do not put a written accent on the **i** or the **u**.

Agudas

Most of the other words in Spanish have the stress on the LAST SYLLABLE. They are called **AGUDAS**. The rules 1. and 2. below are exactly the opposite of the rules for the LLANAS.

Agudas and the written accent (TILDE):

1. An AGUDA ending in a vowel **–s** or **–n**, is written WITH a written accent on the nuclear vowel of the stressed syllable.

mamá	**hindú**	**jamás**	**acordeón**
papá	**Perú**	**explosión**	**montón**
café	**interviú**	**recién**	**preparación**
bebé	**autobús**	**aquí**	**gestión**
así	**hachís**	**bailarín**	**después**
esquí	**compás**	**almacén**	**acción**
israelí	**bantú**	**información**	
emú	**país**	**botón**	

2. An AGUDA ending with a consonant other than **–s** or **–n**, is written WITHOUT a written accent on the nuclear vowel of the stressed syllable: **abril**, **actitud**, **chupachup**, **hablar**, **vivir**, **Paraguay**, etc.
3. Remember that even though the singular of many words ending in **-ín, -én, -ón, -ión**, **-sión**, **-ción,** have a written accent, the same as other AGUDAS that end in **–n,** the plural of these words doesn't have a written accent: **almacenes**, **bailarines**, **montones**, **gestiones**, **explosiones**, **acciones**, **acordeones**, etc. Once you add the syllable **–es**, it becomes a LLANA.
4. Because a **z** is not used as an indicator of person in the conjugation of verbs or the plural of nouns, it is considered a consonant as any other and must not be put in the same category as **s**, even if it

represents the same sound in most of the Spanish speaking world: **veloz**, **feliz**, **eficaz**, **merluz**, **escasez**, etc.

2. There is a written accent in words such as **raíz**, **reír**, **oír**, **baúl**, etc. because the stress is on the **i** and the **u**. The written accent indicates that these are HIATUSES and not diphthongs.

3. The plural of loan words from other languages, for example **esnobs**, **mamuts** are exceptions, because even though they end in **–s**, they have no written accent.

Esdrújulas

All the words that are stressed on the THIRD TO LAST (ANTEPENULT) syllable have a written accent to mark the stressed syllable. Most of them are scholarly words or loan words from other languages:

esdrújula **sábado** **cámara** **pájaro**
básico **agrícola** **década** **artículo**
cómico **académico** **médico** **genérico**

Also, the plurals **jóvenes**, **márgenes**, **imágenes**, **exámenes** and **orígenes** are ESDRÚJULAS while the singular forms are LLANAS.

Sobresdrújulas

There are no words in the dictionary that have the stress on a syllable other than the last, the second to last, or third to last. However, we can find words with a written accent on the fourth to last syllable in texts: ¡Pre-**gún**-ta-me-lo!, ¡**Á**-bre-me-los!, etc. These are word forms consisting of an imperative or a gerund and one or more pronouns at the end.

díganme **cuéntamelo** **gánatela**
póngalas **organízatelo** **cómpranoslas**
díganoslo **repítamelo** **dibújaselos**

Frequent mistakes

1. Many people make a mistake by putting a written accent on top of the **i** in past participles such as **construido**, **huida**, **constituida** etc. This is not necessary because, as we stated in Chapter 1, when there is a combination of two weak vowels in a syllable, it is always the SECOND that gets the stress.
2. Two strong vowels (**a, e, o**) together belong to two syllables and follow the general rules of accentuation: **caos**, **traer**, **mear**, etc.
3. Today, one syllable words are written without accents (with the exception of the diacritic accent): **mes**, **bien**, **fe**, etc. This goes also for monosyllabic verb forms with diphthongs: **fui, fue, dio, vio, hui, crie, crio, fie, fio, frio, guie**, **guio**, **lie**, **pie**, **pio**, **rio**, etc.
4. Before the last orthography reform by the Spanish Royal Language Academy in 1999, the norm was that when a command or another verb form had an accent mark on the last syllable, it was maintained after adding a pronoun, even though the addition would have rendered it obsolete. People, for example wrote **déme**, **dáles**, **díle**, **estáte quieto**, **supónlo**, etc. Today it is assumed that these word forms follow the general rules of accentuation –they are LLANAS– and are therefore written without accents: **deme, dales, dile, estate quieto, suponlo**. Obviously, you must use an accent mark when you add two pronouns to keep the stress on the stem vowels: **démelo**, **dáselo**, **déselo**, **supóntelo**, etc.

The diacritic accent

The diacritic accent is not used to signal the stressed syllable within a word, but to distinguish identical word forms with different meanings that belong to different grammatical categories. This, however, can affect the accentuation in written or spoken texts. (See Chapter 14)

de	PREPOSITION (`from`, `of`): Es el libro de Juan. NOUN (the letter **d**) Domingo se escribe con una de.	**dé**	VERB FORM **DAR**: Es necesario que Ud. me dé su dirección.

el	DEFINITE ARTICLE: El abogado trabaja aquí.	**él**	PERSONAL PRONOUN (he/ him): ¿Quién es? Es él. Hablé con él.
	ADVERSATIVE CONJUNCTION (but, yet): Lo vio, mas no hizo nada.	**más**	ADVERB (more): El caballo corre más rápido que la tortuga. ADJETIVE (more): Juan tiene más hermanos que Carlos. PRONOUN (more) No puedo comer más. IN MATHEMATICS: Uno más uno son dos.
mi	POSSESSIVE ADJECTIVE Es mi libro.	**mí**	PERSONAL PRONOUN El libro es para mí.
se	PRONOUN (himself, herself, themselves): Juan se lava. Aquí se venden periódicos.	**sé**	VERB FORM **SABER**: Yo no sé la hora. VERB FORM **SER**: Sé puntual, por favor.
si	CONJUNCTION (if): Si llueve, nos quedamos aquí.	**sí**	ADVERB (yes): Sí, estoy listo. PERSONAL PRONOUN Ella se ríe de sí misma.
	NOUN (MUSICAL NOTE): Es una melodía en si mayor.		NOUN Triunfó el sí.
te	PERSONAL PRONOUN (you): Te quiero. NOUN (the letter **t**): Tarde se escribe con una te.	**té**	NOUN (tea): El té verde es muy saludable.

tu	POSSESSIVE (your): ¿Es este tu libro?	**tú**	PERSONAL PRONOUN (you): Esto es entre tú y yo.

ATTENTION!

The personal pronoun **ti** is NOT written with an accent mark because the possessive adjective es **tu**: **El libro es de ti**. BUT: Es tu libro.

Question words: adonde/adónde, como/cómo, cual/cuál, cuan/cuán, cuando/cuándo, cuanto/cuánto, donde/dónde, que/qué and quien/quién

The words **adónde**, **cómo**, **cuál**, **cuán**, **cuándo**, **cuánto**, **dónde**, **qué** and **quién** have an accent mark when they are used in questions and exclamations, when they start direct questions (**¿Dónde está tu libro?**) or exclamations (**¡Qué frío hace hoy!**). The same goes for indirect or embedded questions and exclamations (**Pregúntale dónde está su libro. Verás pronto cuánto frío hace hoy.**) The same words are used without an accent mark when they are used as relative pronouns (**Estos son los estudiantes que sacaron un sobresaliente.**), conjunctions (**Yo quiero que me acompañes.**), prepositions (**Te lo digo como hermano.**), adverbs with the meaning of 'around' (**Costó como cien pesos.**), with the meaning of 'por ejemplo' (**Compró muchas cosas como manzanas y peras.**) and in some idiomatic expressions.

Solo, este, ese, aquel

At present, these words are written WITHOUT an accent mark. In the past, to avoid ambiguity, and according to their function within the sentence, they were written with or without an accent mark.

Guion

At present, this and similar words, for example **ion**, **muon**, **prion**, etc. are written WITHOUT an accent mark, independently from how they are pronounced.

Until 1999, these words could be written without an accent mark if they were pronounced with a diphthong **['gjon]** or with an accent mark if they were pronounced with a hiatus **[gi.ˈon]**. In most Spanish speaking countries (including Mexico and Central America) it is pronounced **[ˈgjon]**. In Argentina, Ecuador, Colombia, Venezuela and Spain, preference is given to the form **[gi.ˈon]**.

Aun/aún

The word **aún**, with an accent mark is pronounced as a stressed word with a hiatus [**a.ˈun**] and means **todavía** (**Aún no he dormido**.). The word **aun**, without an accent mark, is an unstressed word with a diphthong that has the meaning of **aunque** (even though) (**Aun cuando diga la verdad, no le creeré.**) **Aun** can be equivalent to **hasta, también, a pesar de** or **incluso** (**Aun los que no estudiaron aprobaron el examen.**)

Words with more than one stress pattern

For several reasons, there is a small number of words with two or even three pronunciations. Most of them are scholarly or loan words from other languages that have conserved their original stress but have also developed parallel Spanish forms that follow the Spanish pronunciation rules. Examples are **olimpíada/ olimpiada**, **período/ periodo**, **alvéolo/alveolo**, **austríaco/ austriaco**, **maníaco/maniaco**, **búmeran/bumerán**, **páprika/ paprika**, **vídeo/video**, **dínamo/dinamo**, **chófer/chofer**, etc. These words are in the middle of a normalization process and can be written according to how they are pronounced by their speakers. It is very likely that the forms without accents will prevail in the future.

Adverbs in -mente

Adverbs that end in **–mente** are the only words in Spanish that have two stressed syllables: **FA-cil-MEN-te**. They maintain the stress of the original adjective and add the stress of **–mente**. When the adjective is written with an accent mark, the adverb as well has an accent mark:

explícita – explícitamente, fácil – fácilmente; débil – débilmente; rápida – rápidamente, básica – básicamente; lógica – lógicamente; etc.

Carácter - espécimen - régimen

Finally, there are three (3) nouns in Spanish that stress a different syllable in their singular and plural forms: **carácter – caracteres; espécimen – especímenes; régimen – regímenes.**

Upper case letters

Even though it is common to find upper case letters written without an accent mark where there should be one, the Spanish Language Academy insists that there is no reason not to use the accent mark.

Questions

1. What is a word?
2. What is a stressed syllable and what is its function?
3. How many stressed syllables are there in Spanish word? Are there exceptions?
4. What are LLANAS?
5. What are AGUDAS?
6. What are ESDRÚJULAS?
7. What is the difference between stress and accent? What is another word for accent in Spanish? How would we translate the English word `stress` into Spanish?
8. What are diphthongs, triphthongs and hiatuses?
9. How do we know that a word is LLANA?
10. How do we know that a word is AGUDA?
11. Where is the stress in the word **escasez**? Do we need an accent?
12. Where is the stress in the word **raiz**? Do we need an accent?
13. How do we know that a word is a ESDRÚJULA? What is the origin of most ESDRÚJULAS? What is the origin of the word **esdrújula**?
14. Do we need an accent mark on the expression **¡Muestramelo!**? Why or why not?
15. Do we need an accent mark on the past participle **distinguido**? Why or why not?
16. Do we need an accent mark on the word **fe**? Why or why not?
17. What is a diacritic accent? What is its function?
18. Do we need an accent mark in the sentences **El libro es de ti.** and **Esto es entre tu y yo.**? Why or why not?
19. Do we need an accent mark in the sentence **Preguntale donde esta su libro.**? Why or why not?
20. Do we need an accent mark in the sentence **Solo me faltan cinco dolares.**? Why or why not?
21. Do we need an accent mark in the sentences **Aun no he dormido.** and **Aun los que no estudiaron aprobaron el examen.**? Why or why not?

22. Do we need an accent mark on the words **paprika** or **video**? Why or why not?
23. Do we need an accent mark on the words **explicitamente** or **her-mosamente**? Why or why not?
24. Do we need an accent mark on the word **regimen** vs. **regimenes**? Why or why not?
25. Do we have to put accent marks on upper case letters?

Exercises

1. **Read the following series of words out loud and apply the rules that you learned in this chapter.** Indicate if the words are **LLANAS (LL), AGUDAS (A), ESDRÚJULAS (E) or SOBRESDRÚJULAS (S)**

☐ ágil	☐ agilizo	☐ agilizó
☐ álabe	☐ alabo	☐ alabó
☐ ánimo	☐ animo	☐ animó
☐ céntrico	☐ centrismo	☐ centralizó
☐ estímulo	☐ estimulo	☐ estimuló
☐ examen	☐ examino	☐ examinó
☐ excavo	☐ excavó	☐ excavación
☐ exprés	☐ expreso	☐ expresó
☐ éxito	☐ excito	☐ excitó
☐ germen	☐ germinan	☐ germinó
☐ régimen	☐ regimientan	☐ regimentaron
☐ santo	☐ santísimo	☐ santoral
☐ sílaba	☐ silabeo	☐ silabación
☐ símil	☐ similar	☐ similitud
☐ síntoma	☐ sintomático	☐ sintomatología
☐ útil	☐ utilizo	☐ utilizó
☐ término	☐ termino	☐ terminó
☐ público	☐ publicó	☐ publicación
☐ manda	☐ mandato	☐ mandamiento
☐ mándamela	☐ explico	☐ explicó
☐ explicación	☐ explícanoslo	

2. **The following words can be pronounced in two ways. Read the following series of words out loud and apply the rules that you learned in this chapter.** Indicate if the words are **LLANAS, AGUDAS, ESDRÚJULAS or SOBRESDRÚJULAS: esdrújula/llana (e/ll), esdrújula/aguda (e/a), llana/aguda (ll/a), llana/esdrújula (ll/e), aguda/llana (a/ll), aguda/esdrújula (a/e).**

- ☐ olimpíada/ olimpiada
- ☐ período/ periodo
- ☐ alvéolo/ alveolo
- ☐ austríaco/ austriaco
- ☐ maníaco/ maniaco
- ☐ búmeran/ bumerán
- ☐ páprika/ paprika
- ☐ vídeo/ video
- ☐ dínamo/ dinamo,
- ☐ chófer/ chofer
- ☐ aloe/ áloe
- ☐ cenit/ cénit
- ☐ polígloto/ poligloto
- ☐ demoníaco/ demoniaco
- ☐ zodiaco/ zodíaco
- ☐ etíope/ etiope
- ☐ fútbol/ futbol
- ☐ íbero/ ibero
- ☐ pedíatra/ pediatra
- ☐ paradisíaco/ paradisiaco
- ☐ utopia/ utopía

3. The main character of the short story "El vocabulario de los balcones" by the Spanish writer Almudena Grandes says that she has used a lot of 'esdrújulas'. **Underline the esdrújulas and add an accent mark where necessary.** We have also omitted the diacritic accent on some words where it is needed. **Underline these words with a different color and add the diacritic accents** (Almudena Grandes, *Modelos de mujer*. Tusquets Editores, S.A., 1996, pages 154/55).

"Averiguar que enseñaba exactamente resultó un poco mas dificil, porque mi interlocutora solo recordaba que su especialidad empezaba por A [...] y lo primero que se me ocurrió fue arquitectura -¡no, mujer, quita ya ...! Tan importante no es-, y luego pregunté si era abogado -¡pero ¿que dices? ¡No, no ... Mucho mas importante que eso- y así, por su peculiar escala de prestigio, fui descartando aparejador, ATS, alergologo, ingeniero aeronautico, aeroespacial y agronomo, arqueologo, filologo alemán, astronomo, astrofisico, y no se cuantas esdrujulas mas.

-¡Si, mujer! -insistió al final-. Si tu tienes que saber lo que es. Hasta salen en la tele de vez en cuando hablando de los salvajes y eso ...

Comprendí enseguida lo que quería decir, pero tardé unos segundos en arrancar a hablar, como si aquella posibilidad me resultara mas inverosimil que algunas de las que yo misma había propuesto, y no pude evitar que me temblara un poco la voz en la primera silaba.

-¿An-tro-po-lo-go? - pregunté muy despacio, casi con miedo y Conchita elevó las dos manos al cielo mientras profería un alarido de triunfo.

-¡Justo!"

Write down the 'esdrújulas' here. Don't forget to use the accents! Spell them the way the author did: 'an-tro-po-lo-go'.

1 ______________________________
2 ______________________________
3 ______________________________
4 ______________________________
5 ______________________________
6 ______________________________
7 ______________________________
8 __es-drú-ju-las______________________
9 ______________________________
10 ______________________________
11 ______________________________

Write down the words that carry a diacritic accent and indicate their grammatical function. List also the repetitions.

Word Grammatical category

1 ______________________________
2 ______________________________
3 ______________________________
4 ______________________________
5 ______________________________
6 ______________________________
7 ______________________________
8 ______________________________
9 ______________________________
10 ______________________________

There are also two 'llanas' in the text that need accents. These words are

________________________________ and

________________________________ .

4. Esdrújulas: Find and write down the following Spanish words:

Horizontal:

2 A person that belongs to the bureaucracy (a public servant) is a **b...a**

3 The science that studies plants is called **b...a**

5 Words can be divided into smaller units. They are called **s...s**

7 Someone who is very active and has a lot of energy is **d...o**

8 Someone who has bronchitis is **b...o**

9 Science dealing with the identification of the substances of which matter is composed; the investigation of their properties and the ways in which they interact, combine, and change and that uses formulas such as H_2O is called **q...a**

Vertical:

1 The noun that corresponds to the verb 'buscar' is b...**a**

2 The adjective that goes with 'biología' es **b...o**

4 A man living in Bulgaria is a **b ...o**

6 A man who has bulimia is **b...o**

5. Add the accent marks where they belong.

articulo
articulacion
articulado
binoculo
calculo
circulo
corpusculo
crepusculo
cubiculo
espectacular
grupusculo
masculo
mayusculo
meticulosamente
miraculoso

6. Add the accent marks where they belong.

bahia
vehiculo
exhibir
te prohibo
inhabil
La Habana
antiheroe
rehen
alcoholico
inhospito
prohibicion

7. Singular/Plural: Put the accents where they belong.

autobus/ autobuses	algun/ algunos
hollin/ hollines	automovil/ automoviles
caiman/ caimanes	especimen/especimenes
tension/ tensiones	jamon/ jamones
caracter/ caracteres	catalan/ catalanes
rey/ reyes	esdrujula/ esdrujulas
pais/ paises	imagen/ imagenes
regimen/ regimenes	registro/ registros
capitan/ capitanes	violin/ violines
invalido/ invalidos	comun/ comunes
joven/ jovenes	aleman/ alemanes
jardin/ jardines	volcan/ volcanes

8. Question words and diacritics: Put the accents where they belong.

1 No se que quieres de mi.

2 Se que el no esta enfermo.

3 Me pregunto que quiere de el.

4 ¿Cual es tu libro?

5 ¿Por qué quieres que el te de su nombre?

6 ¿Cuándo el me va a dar mas dinero?

7 El libro no es de el, es de mi.

8 Mi padre es mas tranquilo que mi hermano.

9 No se si hay mas tiempo.

10 Creo que sí, que esta enfermo.

11 Ella se ríe de si misma.

12 Aun queda una tasa de te.

13 Aun cuando venga mas tarde, con quiero saber nada de el.

14 Te dije que quiero mas te.

15 No pensaba eso de ti.

16 Se adonde va mañana.

17 Me pregunto donde estuvo ayer.

18 Vendré cuando pueda.

19 Yo se quien bebió el te.

20 ¡Que pena que no bebas te!

21 No se como lo hiciste.

22 El libro cuesta como cien dólares.

23 Solo me falta el.

9. Adverbs: Add accent marks where they belong.

actualmente
agilmente
alegoricamente
altamente
amablemente
analogamente
aproximadamente
artisticamente
basicamente
catastroficamente
celosamente
ciegamente
comodamente
criticamente
debilmente
deliciosamente
doblemente
epicamente
esporadicamente
explicitamente
facilmente
graciosamente
habilmente
higienicamente
logicamente
particularmente
practicamente
rapidamente
realmente
sistematicamente

10. The following words are stressed on the syllables containing the bolded vowels. Add accent marks where they belong.

Agust**i**n
alt**a**r
an**e**cdotas
ang**e**licos
apice
aqu**i**
aristot**e**lico
armon**i**a
ben**e**volas
b**i**blico
c**e**lebre
cl**e**rigo
cl**e**rigos
com**u**n
connotaci**o**n
constru**i**da
contempor**a**nea
dep**o**sito
despu**e**s
dial**e**ctico
di**a**logo
difer**e**nte
din**a**mica
dor**a**da

du**e**ña
ecos
Ed**e**n
epoca
esp**e**cie
espec**i**fico.
espor**a**dico
esquem**a**tico
esquem**a**ticos
est**a**
est**a**ticas
estr**e**cha
etc**e**tera
etimol**o**gicas
eval**u**a
evang**e**lica
exeg**e**sis
expl**i**citamente
f**a**ciles
fig**u**ra
folkl**o**rico
f**o**nicamente
f**o**rja
form**a**ndo

forzar**a**n (fut.)
fr**i**o
gen**e**ricos
g**e**neros
gr**a**cias
guill**e**n
h**a**bil
hagiogr**a**ficas
herm**o**sa
h**e**roes
hist**o**rico
hom**e**ricos
im**a**gen
im**a**genes
imp**u**dico
instrum**e**nto
inter**e**s
in**u**tilm**e**nte
jer**a**rquico
jud**i**os
jur**i**dico
l**a**na
lat**i**n
le**o**n

l**i**nea
l**i**quido
lit**u**rgicas
lit**u**rgico
ll**a**mas
l**o**gico
lug**a**r
m**a**dre
manten**e**r
Mar**i**a
mart**i**llo
m**a**rtires
Men**e**ndez
m**e**rito
met**a**foras
metaf**o**ricas
miniat**u**ras
mon**a**stica
muj**e**r
ning**u**n
n**u**cleos
n**u**mero

ordenes
organo
pa**i**s
pa**i**ses
Para**i**so
patr**i**stica
pir**a**mide
po**e**tico
port**a**tiles
pres**e**ntes
proteg**i**do
p**u**blico
quiz**a**s
reci**e**n
recu**e**rda
rel**a**to
repres**e**nta
ret**o**ricos
rev**e**s
rom**a**nico
r**u**brica
sem**a**nticos

serm**o**n
simb**o**lica
simil**a**res
sit**u**a
sovi**e**tica
subr**a**ya
s**u**plica
tambi**e**n
t**e**cnica
Te**o**filo
teol**o**gica
te**o**logo
t**e**rminos
unica
utilitar**i**smo
v**e**anse
veh**i**culo
v**i**rgen
v**i**rgenes
visi**o**n
vu**e**lve
f**a**cilmente

11. Read the following text and add accent marks where necessary. The bold-faced vowels in some nouns, verb forms and other words that you may not know, mark the stressed syllables. You can listen to a recording of the text on the book's Web site.

La Guantanamera es una de las canciones más famosas del mundo. El cantante habanero Jos**e**ito Fern**a**ndez la compuso un incierto dia de 1928. Era durante el regimen de Ger**a**rdo Mach**a**do, uno de los lideres de los regimenes corruptos que se sucedieron en el pais. El compositor no soñ**o** con que medio siglo despues su cancion se convert**i**ria en un autentico himno de Cuba. Joseito y *La Guantanamera* fueron, gracias al cantante norteamericano Pete Seeger, quien la populariz**o** en la d**e**cada de los sesenta, los precurs**o**res del gran boom internacional que la musica popular cubana vive en nuestros dias.

Seeger pens**o** que era una cancion de caracter folcl**o**rico. Le puso estrofas de varios *Versos sencillos* de Jos**e** Mart**i**: *"Yo soy un hombre sincero/ de donde crece la palma/ y antes de morirme quiero/ echar mis versos del alma"*, y la cancion empez**o** a rodar por todo el mundo. Luego vinieron las versiones del trio californiano The Sandpipers y del frances Joe Dassin, y *La Guantanamera* se convirti**o** en una mina de oro.

Ajeno a este exito y a los derechos de autor, no fue hasta mil novecientos setenta y uno que Joseito Fernandez le pudo contar a Seeger la verdadera historia de la cancion. Joseito muri**o** el once de octubre de mil novecientos setenta y nueve, sin ahorros ni lujos, aunque al menos su nombre qued**o** grabado en la historia de la musica cubana y mundial.

5

The vowel phonemes /a/, /e/, /i/, /o/, /u/

You have already learned in Chapter 1 that the difference between a consonant and vowels is that, for consonants, the airflow is always obstructed, and that vowels come out of the mouth without any kind of obstruction. Vowels are also part of a group of sounds called **CONTINUANTS** without friction because there is an uninterrupted flow of air that comes out of the mouth (or the nose, in other languages). Other non-vocalic continuants are [f, l, m, n, s, v], among others.

There is a small group of sounds that occupy a position in between vowels and consonants that are called semi-vowels (or semi-consonants) or **GLIDES** [j] and [w].

The vowel system of Spanish is rather simple and consists of only five (5) basic vowels, **a**, **e**, **i**, **o**, **u**, and eight (8) **DIPHTHONGS**, combinations of two vowels: **a**, **e**, **o** + **i** or **u**; or **i** + **u** vs. **u** + **i**; and some **TRIPHTHONGS**, combinations of the vowels **i**/ **u** + **a**/ **e**/ **o** + **i**/ **u**. (See Chapter 1)

The quality and length of a vowel sound is generally the same in all phonetic contexts, whether a vowel is stressed or not.

The vowel system of English, on the other hand, is more complex and intricate than in Spanish. Furthermore, there is more geographical variation in English vowels. Many vowel sounds in English are diphthongs, for example the sounds [eɪ] and [oʊ] in `bait`, `made`, `sow`, `coat`, `rode`. (As you can see in the spelling of the examples, the diphthongs in English are not limited to the combination of two different graphemes, as it is the case in Spanish, but can also be written with a single vowel, **a** or **o**.) This is the reason why many Americans pronounce words such as **yo** and **José** → *[ɟow] and *[xow.'zej] instead of [ɟo] and [xo.'se]. Another problem is that many vowels that exist in the English language, are nonexistent in Spanish, for example [æ] in Engl. bat. The most important is the **SCHWA** sound, represented in the phonetic transcription with the symbol [ə]. It represents a mid central unstressed vowel, for example in the English words about [ə.'baʊt], supply [sə.'plaɪ] or episode [ɛ.pə.soʊd]. Applying the phonological system of English to Spanish produces the typical American accent that we are trying to avoid if we want to acquire a more authentic Spanish pronunciation. Therefore, we must avoid pronouncing the vowels **a**, **e**, **o** as diphthongs, shorten the vowels **i** and **u**, and not use sounds that do not exist in Spanish.

In the next chapter, we will explain the three (3) types of information that we must know to describe a consonant, which are:

1. sonority: if it is voiced or unvoiced
2. place of articulation
3. manner of articulation

To describe a vowel, we also need three (3) types of information, that are different and not so precise.

1. First, **TONGUE BACKNESS**, whether the vowel is articulated in the FRONT, the CENTER, or the BACK of the mouth (in Spanish: ANTERIOR, CENTRAL, or POSTERIOR).
2. Second, **TONGUE HEIGHT**, the elevation or vertical position of the tongue in the mouth, i.e. whether the vowel is LOW, MID, or HIGH (in Spanish: BAJA, MEDIA or ALTA).
3. Finally, we need to identify the **ROUNDEDNESS** of the lips, whether they are **SPREAD** as in ee of beet) (in Spanish: ESTIRADO); **NEUTRAL** or relaxed, when you are saying ah; or **ROUNDED** (in Spanish: REDONDEADO), for example oo in soon.

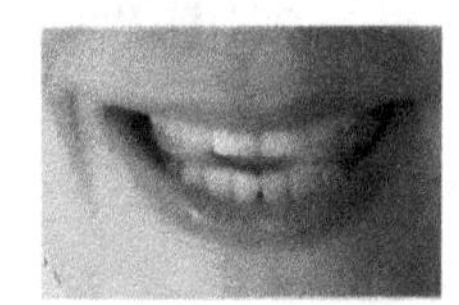

spread

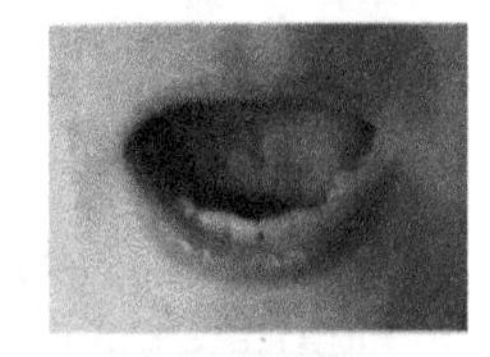

neutral

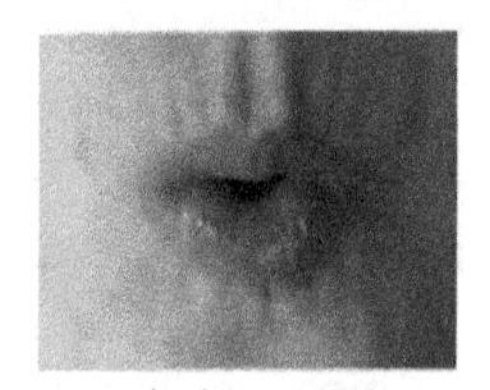

rounded

In Spanish, the [a] of casa, for example, is a low, central, and neutral vowel; the [e] of pelo is a mid, front, spread vowel; the [u] of uno is a high, back, rounded vowel.

To summarize, there are three kinds of information that we must know to define a vowel sound:

1. TONGUE BACKNESS ↔: FRONT, CENTER, or BACK
2. TONGUE HEIGHT ↕: LOW, MID, or HIGH
3. Lip ROUNDEDNESS: NEUTRAL, SPREAD, ROUNDED

Visualization of the articulation of vowels

Types of vowel sounds

There are two (2) kinds of vowel sounds:

1. Pure or full vowels
2. Semi-vowels or glides

The pure/full vowels start and finish the same way. The five (5) basic vowels in Spanish are all pure vowels.

GLIDES (Span. **DESLIZADAS**) or **SEMI-VOWELS** (Span. **SEMIVOCALES**), the sounds [j] and [w], are always combined with pure vowels to form **DIPHTHONGS** (for example in **hacia** and **deuda**) or **TRIPHTHONGS** (for example in **Paraguay**). They are called glides because they "glide" from one point of articulation to another. The glides can precede or follow the pure vowel. In **hacia**, for example, the diphthong starts high in the front of the mouth and glides immediately towards the [a], that is neutral and central. In **deuda**, the diphthong starts with the pure vowel [e] and glides to the [w] sound that is pronounced high in the back of the mouth. Spanish has five (5) pure vowels, two (2) glides and many diphthongs (combinations of pure vowels and glides). (More information in Chapter 1.)

The vocalic phonemes of Spanish

/a/

[a] **PURE VOWEL: CENTRAL, LOW, NEUTRAL**

In any position: **alma**, **casa**, **caigo**, **caída**, **causa**, **caer**, etc.

/e/

[e] **PURE VOWEL: FRONT, MID, SPREAD**

In any position: **ese**, **creer**, **duermen**, **deuda**, **hablé**, **nadie**, etc.

/i/

[i] **PURE VOWEL: FRONT, HIGH, SPREAD**

i at the beginning of words + consonant: **istmo**, **invierno**, **hito**, etc.

i between vowels: **dime**, **risa**, etc.

i after **u** as second letter of a diphthong: **cuidado**, **huir**, etc.

i with accent in any position: **corrí**, **maní**, **hígado**, **frío**, **hacía**, **ríe**, etc.

[j] **GLIDE: FRONT, HIGH, SPREAD** (See Chapter 1)

i without an accent mark BEFORE or AFTER **a**, **e**, **o** (in diphthongs and triphthongs): **hielo**, **miel**, **especie**, **dio**, **miau**, **baile**, **aceite**, **oigo**, **guay**, etc.

i before **u** as first letter of a diphthong: **ciudad**, **viuda**, etc.

y at the end of words: **estoy**, **hay**, **ley**, etc./o/

/o/

[o] **PURE VOWEL: BACK, MID, ROUNDED**

in any position: **onda**, **coco**, **amo**, **loquísimo**, **cósmico**, **color**, etc.

/u/

[u] PURE VOWEL: BACK, HIGH, ROUNDED

at the beginning of words + consonant: **usted**, **uva**, **uso**, etc.

between consonants: **abuso**, **buscar**, etc.

at the end of words after consonants: **Perú**, **espíritu**, etc.

u after **i** as second letter of a diphthong: **ciudad**, **viuda**, etc.

with accent in any position: **atún**, **aún**, **continúa**, **interviú**, **veintiún**, etc.

[w] GLIDE: BACK, HIGH, ROUNDED (See Chapter 1)

u without an accent mark, before or after **a**, **e**, **o** (in diphthongs and triphthongs): **fue**, **aula**, **agua**, **cuota**, **guardar**, **deuda**, **aula**, **estadounidense**, **miau**, etc.

u before **i** as first letter of a diphthong: **cuidado**, **hui**, etc.

American English vowels

The following list represents what is called the "Broadcast pronunciation," which attempts to describe a neutral, accent-free pronunciation, which in reality does not exist. Some people say that the American English spoken in the mid-west of the US is the most neutral. Without judging any of the varieties of English spoken in the US, in what follows, we will try to give a description of such a neutral form because it would go far beyond the scope of this book if we tried to list all the variations.

There are five (5) vowels that are always diphthongs, as well as ten (10) pure vowels and three (3) glides.

The diphthongs

bait [eɪ]

bite [aɪ]

boat [oʊ]

bout [aʊ]

boy [ɔɪ]

* [ɪ] and [ʊ] are vocalic sounds in English that are very similar to the glides [j] and [w] in Spanish.

In addition to these diphthongs, in different English dialects, the long vowels are diphthongs as well, even though they are only written with one vowel.

beet [ij]

boot [uw]

Look in the mirror when you pronounce these words and check to see if your lips move when you pronounce the vowels. If they do, even if it is only a little bit, when you pronounce **ee** and **oo**, then they are likely diphthongs. The other diphthongs are more obvious and unavoidable in English: [eɪ], [oʊ]. Therefore, when Americans learn Spanish, very naturally and unavoidably, the word **de** will sound like [deɪ] and **hablo** like ['a.βloʊ], because they do not have another way to pronounce e and o at the end of a word.

It requires a lot of practice to eliminate the glides at the end of words that are caused by interference with English. So, how can this be achieved? Here is one suggestion: Because glides are always very short and tacked on to the end of the diphthongs, one thing that you can do is keep the first part of the diphthong very long: [eeeeeeeeeeej]. Then repeat the sound but cut the long [eeeeeeeeeee] into many short pure vowels and use the [j] only after the last [e] → [e-e-e-e-e-e-e-e-ej]. Finally, drop the [j] at the end → [e-e-e-e-e-e-e-e-ej]. You can do the same exercise with a final o that tends to sound like [ow]: [oooooooooooow] → [o-o-o-o-o-o-o-o-o-o-o-ow] → [o-o-o-o-o-o-o-o-o-o-o-o].

The monophthongs

bet [ɛ]

bat [æ]

bit [ɪ]

bot [ɑ]

but [ʌ]

bought [ɔ]

book [ʊ]

burn [ɚ]

complimentary, duplicate (noun), photograph, excellent [ə]

The following series represents pure vowels, some of which will surprise you:

The vowel [ɚ] is only used before the [r] sound. The most surprising thing is that in the combination **ur**, such as in `burn`, the American **r** becomes a **RHOTACIZED** vowel instead of a consonant. The sound leaves the mouth without any kind of friction or interference, and this is the reason why it can count as a vowel. The combination er in British English, such as in `father`, that sounds almost identical to the a sound: ['fɑ.ðɑ], is clearly a vowel as well.

The use of the American **r** in Spanish is a giveaway because it reveals that you are probably an American or Canadian. Even though the consonant sound [ɾ] exists in English, it is difficult for English speakers to apply to **r** due to a different phonological distribution in English than in Spanish. On the other hand, of course, it is also difficult for non-native English speakers to pronounce the American **r** because there is no equivalent in any of the European languages.

The last vowel on the list, the [ə], known as **SCHWA**, can also affect your pronunciation in Spanish. In English, any unstressed vowel can sound like [ə], as you can see in the examples complimentary, `duplicate` (noun), `photograph` and **excellent** above. In Spanish, on the other hand, all the vowels are pronounced in the same way, no matter if they are stressed or unstressed. Therefore, it is imperative to articulate them very clearly and not to reduce or modify the unstressed vowels. In English, `Alabama` is pronounced [æ.lə.'bæ.mə], but in Spanish, the four **as** in **alababa** are all pronounced the same way: [a.la.'βa.βa].

Because there are so many vowels in English, you may think that Spanish and English share many of the same sounds, but when you compare the two systems, you will see that they only share the [a] sound and sometimes [i] and [u]. All the other sounds may need a lot of practice.

Exercises

The phoneme /a/

1. **Read the first part of the Balada para Amanda Argañaraz, written by A. G. Corbella and published in the *Revista Tía Vicenta* (Buenos Aires), year VIII, number 281, may 1964, in which the author only uses the vowel a.**

Acá van las palabras más francas para alabar a Amanda Argañaraz, alma arrastrada a la Nada tras la más malhadada batalla para alcanzar a amar al canalla más falaz; batalla parada tras larga zaranda para acabar abrazada a la Parca, arrastrada al mar.

¡Acallad las amargas palabras!

¡Paz para Amanda Argañaraz!

Amanda Argañaraz amaba la campaña: largaba las frazadas a la blanda cama al aclarar cada alba anaranjada.

Lavaba la cara, bajaba a la planta baja; para halagar a la mamá, cantaba raras baladas, tras sacar para yantar las tajadas más bastas a las manzanas, a las naranjas, a las bananas, a las granadas. Calzaba blancas alpargatas; calaba bata asargada, calzas batarazas, ancha faja, alba casaca, gabán calamar, pardas gafas. Apartaba la más mansa asna a la majada, atábala, cabalgábala, lanzaba la jaca alazana para vagar tras las cabañas más apartadas. Mas la dama jamás maltrataba la asna: Amanda amaba la jaca, tan mansa, tan llana, tan flaca ...

2. **There is also a text by Rubén Darío that only uses the vowel a. Read the beginning of this text.**

AMAR HASTA FRACASAR

Faltaba ya nada para anclar; mas la mar brava, lanza a la playa la fragata: la vara. Arranca tablas al tajamar; nada basta a salvar la fragata. (Ah, tantas almas lanzadas al mar, ya agarradas a tablas claman, ya nadan para ganar la playa! Blas nada para acá, para allá, para hallar a Ana, para salvarla. (Ah, tantas brazadas, tan gran afán para nada. Hállala, mas la halla ya matada! ¡¡¡Matada!!! ... Abraza a la amada: -¡Amar hasta fracasar! – clama ...

3. Now read the following recipe to practice the vowel a.

<u>Calabaza asada</u>

INGREDIENTES:

1 libra de calabaza
6 cucharadas de leche
5 cucharadas de harina de Castilla
3 huevos
1/8 libra de mantequilla
1 ramita de perejil
1 cucharadita de sal
1/8 cucharadita de pimienta

PREPARACIÓN:

Se pela y se limpia de semillas la calabaza, cortándola en pedazos medianos. Se polvorean con pimienta molida, se rebozan y se fríen; se colocan en una cacerola plana o sartén grande. Se baten los huevos con la leche y la sal y se vierte sobre la calabaza. Se hornea durante media hora o se cocina en la olla de presión hasta que se ablande la calabaza. Se adorna con perejil, o si se prefiere con anillos de cebolla, tiras de ají pimiento asado o queso rallado.

4. Read the following children's rhyme.

Brujas, brujitas y brujotas con brazos largos y medias rotas.

Abracadabra!

Patas de cabra!

Brotan embrujos en cada palabra.

Brujas sin dientes

¿Dónde estarán?

Si yo toco el timbre ... ¿me abrirán?

5. Read the following palindromes (words and phrases that are identical if you read them from the left to right or right to left).

Aman a Panamá
Ana, la tacaña catalana.
Atar a la rata.
Amad a la dama.
Ana lava lana.
Anita lava la tina

The phoneme /e/

6. First practice the [e].

beca	dejo	meta	seda
besa	esa	neta	seta
beso	geta	pelo	tela
beta	jefa	peso	tema
ceja	jeta	peta	vega
cero	leña	rema	velo
dedo	letra	seca	veta

7. The e at the end of a word often causes problems, because English speakers tend to pronounce them as diphthongs [ej]. Read the following words and try to avoid the diphthongs.

abre	cree	fase	ríe
aire	dame	fue	trae
arde	debe	hace	une
ave	efe	lave	uve
base	eje	lee	hablé
bebe	ene	Noé	conté
cae	ere	olé	
come	ese	que	

8. Read the following palindromes.

Échele leche
ser tres
Sé verle del revés
Se es o no se es

The phoneme /i/

9. Read the following examples, all with a stressed i.

ahí	aquí	esquí	jabalí	rubí
ají	ceutí	frenesí	mambí	si
así	colibrí	iraní	Martí	ti
caí	coquí	iraquí	mi	vi
alfonsí	di	israelí	nací	

10. The unstressed i in the following examples becomes the semi-vowel [j]. Read the examples.

aliado	bien	reina	coincide
aria	gaita	seis	estoico
Asia	ciego	veinte	oiga
odiar	cielo	dio	heroico
triada	cien	dios	Celsius
baile	diez	kiosco	ciudad
fraile	piel	miocardio	triunfa
Cairo	Ceiba	miope	veintiuno
naipe	peine	boina	viuda

The phoneme /o/

11. Spanish speakers may identify you as an American if you pronounce the Spanish o as [ow], especially a stressed o at the end of syllable or word. In English, there is either a consonant at the end or one of the three glides. Try to pronounce the following words with a short tense o, without a glide.

no	dio	ufo	leyó	loco
yo	mío	uno	bosque	robo
ajo	cojo	uso	bajó	rojo
amo	loro	mosca	cayó	roto
amó	pozo	veo	curó	
año	oyó	habló	bobo	
asó	los	pensó	como	
coco	tío	miró	foro	

12. Read the first part of a song by León Gieco in which he only uses the vowel o.

Ojo con los Orozco

(CORO): Nosotros no somos como los Orozco,

yo los conozco son ocho los monos:

Pocho, Toto, Cholo, Tom, Moncho, Rodolfo, Otto, Pololo.

Yo pongo los votos sólo por Rodolfo,

los otros son locos, yo los conozco,

no los soporto. ¡Stop! ¡Stop!

¡Pocho Orozco!

Odontólogo ortodoxo, doctor.

Como Bolocotó, oncólogo jodón.

Morocho, tordo, groncho, jocoso, trosco,

chocó con los montos. Colocó molotov.

¡Bonzo!

¡Stop! ¡Stop!

13. Read the following palindromes with the vowel o.

O dolor o lodo	Ojo rojo
Somos o no somos	Oro moro

The phoneme /u/

14. The /u/ in Spanish is short and is not a diphthong. Read the following words

bus	club	ataúd	común
luz	cruz	astur	Jesús
sub	plus	atún	salud
sur	algún	aún	según
sus	almud	azul	virtud
tus	alud	baúl	avestruz

15. Now read the unstressed u in the following examples.

álbum	butaca	fulano	lujoso
cactus	cubano	fumar	mucoso
campus	culebra	gusano	nuboso
casus	cuñado	jugaba	mulato
cónsul	curado	jugoso	sujeto
corpus	dudoso	jurado	rutina

16. An unstressed u next to e, o, and a before i becomes the semi-vowel [w].

cuasi	cuota	neuma	pausa	reuma
cuate	bueno	cuida	Ceuta	fauna
guapa	cuero	huida	cuota	deuda
Juana	duele	ruido	jaula	asiduo
cauce	huele	suizo	feudo	pausa
suave	fuera	ruina	muere	

Final exercise

17. Read the following sentences (taken from newspaper articles) aloud, paying close attention to the pronunciation of vowels.

a. Naseiro acudió acompañado de su hija, que con gestos visibles le indicaba que se calmara, que no insistiera en una declaración o alababa sus palabras.

b. Una mujer de avanzada edad no se atrevía a darle la mano, detalle que advirtió la hija de los Reyes, que se acercó a saludarla, mientras la anciana le alababa su belleza.

c. Las alteraciones de este tipo se expresan en un lenguaje asintáctico y, por tanto, en muchos casos se llega a la agramaticalidad. Aquí ha lugar la distinción de Chomsky entre aceptabilidad y competencia. Una frase es aceptable si, aun incumpliendo las reglas sintácticas, conserva la posibilidad de transmitir su sentido.

d. Este queso se caracteriza por su forma esférica, con protección antiparasitaria de cera roja exterior. Se fabrica también en España.

e. La sensación de estar caminando atrás en el tiempo era demasiado avasalladora como para dejar fisuras al presente inmediato. Nada de lo que estaba viendo, se le ocurría, pertenecía al presente. Esa naturaleza estaba muerta, y su orden pertenecía a un pasado lejano, sibilinamente infiltrado en su modo de percibir la realidad.

f. Es cierto que se trataba de una figura de la vida policíaca bajacaliforniana que no sólo había investigado la muerte de José Federico Benítez López. Además, tenía en su haber un número importante de averiguaciones y asuntos que lo colocaban como potencial blanco de un número importante, significativo, de pasiones que este fin de semana terminaron por desbordarse segando su vida.

g. Los ex-rebeldes iniciaron la entrega del armamento colectivo utilizado en el marco del conflicto armado interno, acto en el cual destacaron ametralladoras, lanzagranadas y artefactos explosivos.

h. A través de la frontera con Honduras funcionaba eficientemente un correo con la ciudad de Danlí.

i. Cuando algunos escritores llamados vernáculos utilizaron en nuestro país el tema del indio, el tema del campesino, lo estaban haciendo siempre desde una perspectiva eminentemente elitista.

j. La nueva cultura que debemos construir en Nicaragua tiene que ser una cultura de hondo contenido popular, tiene que ser una cultura eminentemente popular.

k. Las manos del mulato criollo aprendieron a tocar eficientemente no sólo la bandurria y la guitarra sino también el acordeón y el arpa.

l. El arte sirve aquí para embellecer, ennoblecer y dignificar no ya una iglesia o un palacio, sino un gran hotel. Teóricamente, la operación consiste en exponer el arte donde está el público, sin esperar a que éste vaya a su encuentro.

m. Se entiende por retórica al arte del bien decir, de embellecer la expresión de los conceptos, de dar al lenguaje escrito o hablado eficacia para deleitar, persuadir o conmover.

n. Asimismo, la imprescriptibilidad significa que el dominio directo es a perpetuidad, no prescribe nunca.

o. En tal escenario encontramos la revocatoria del poder político, la elección de magistrados de la Función Judicial, la institucionalización de la Comisión Anticorrupción de contralor y fiscal, la institucionalización de la Comisión Anticorrupción, etc.

p. La ministerial debe gozar del don de la invisibilidad, porque nadie en Palmar de Ocoa se atreve a asegurar que ella dice la verdad.

q. Usufructo y uso: El carácter vitalicio de estos derechos reales menores determina que la titularidad de los mismos se extinga con la muerte del usufructuario o usuario y, además, estos derechos no son transmisibles por causa de muerte.

r. Para ello parte de la definición de “denotativo” como el conjunto de las informaciones que vehicula una unidad lingüística y que le permiten entrar en relación con un objeto extra-lingüístico, durante los procesos onomasiológico (denominación) y semasiológico (extracción de sentido e identificación del referente).

6
Consonants

The characteristics of consonants

As you know and as we have explained in Chapter 1, we distinguish **VOWELS** (**a, e, i, o, u**) and **CONSONANTS**. A vowel comes out of the mouth with nothing getting in the way. When you say ah! or ee!, or any other vowel sound in any language, it flows out of your mouth unimpeded. A consonant, on the other hand, is a sound that has some impediment or obstruction that squeezes, stops, or reroutes the sound before it leaves the mouth. **GLIDES** are in between consonants and vowels.

The next several lessons are going to deal with the Spanish consonants, how they are produced, how they contrast with the English consonants, and how you can overcome the stumbling blocks caused by interference from English consonants when you are pronouncing Spanish. Before you begin the following chapters you need to know three (3) things in order to explain (or understand) how a consonant is produced:

- the **PLACE OF ARTICULATION** (Span. **PUNTO DE ARTICULACIÓN**) (where in the mouth the sound is produced and where the obstruction occurs)
- the **MANNER OF ARTICULATION** (Span. **MODO DE ARTICULACIÓN**) (how the sound is produced)
- **VOICING,** if the sound is **VOICED** or **UNVOICED** (Span. **SONORIDAD**; si el sonido es **SORDO** o **SONORO**)

The articulatory system: Anatomy of the vocal tract

1. the ORAL CAVITY (Span. la cavidad oral)
2. the LIPS (Span. los labios)
a. the UPPER LIP (Span. el labio superior)
b. the LOWER LIP (Span. el labio inferior)
3. the TEETH (Span. los dientes)
4. the ALVEOLAR RIDGE (Span. los alvéolos)
5. the HARD PALATE (Span. el paladar)
6. the VELUM or SOFT PALATE (Span. el velo del paladar)
7. the UVULA (Span. la úvula)
8. the TONGUE (Span. la lengua)
    a. the TIP of the tongue (Span. el ápice de la lengua)
    b. the FRONT (Span. el predorso)
    c. the CENTER (Span. el dorso)
    d. the BACK (Span. el postdorso)
    e. the ROOT (Span. la raíz)
9. the PHARYNX (Span. la cavidad faringe)
10. the EPIGLOTTIS (Span. el epiglotis)
11. the LARYNX with the GLOTTIS and the VOCAL CORDS (Span. la laringe con la glotis y las cuerdas vocales)
12. the NASAL CAVITY (Span. la cavidad nasal)
13. the NOSE (Span. la nariz)

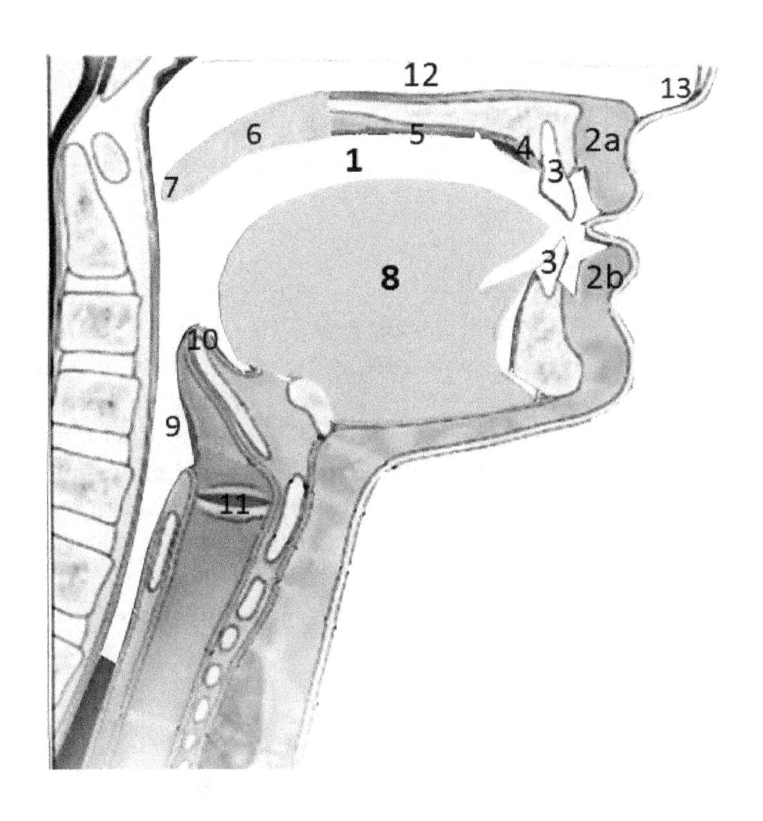
12
13
6
5
4
2a
1
3
7
8
3
2b
10
9
11

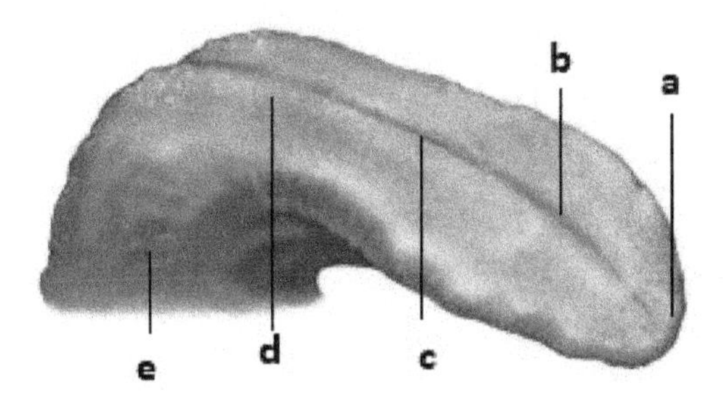
b
a
e
d
c

Place of articulation

First, it is necessary to know the PLACE OF ARTICULATION (Span. punto de articulación) of a consonant, which is the point in the mouth where the sound is produced. A consonant can be

BILABIAL

The consonants **m**, **p,** and **b**, for example, are all articulated with your upper and lower lips. They are all **BILABIAL** sounds. Your two lips close completely when you produce **m**. This is called occlusion (See below under 'manner of articulation'). The air and the resulting sound come out of the nose. The same goes for **n** and **ñ**. (See below under 'manner of articulation') For **b** and **p,** the lips are also closed when the sound is formed, and the flow of air is blocked. In this case, however, the air does not escape through the nose, because after the pressure in the mouth has reached a certain level, the speaker opens the lips and the air bursts out of the mouth. The difference between **b** and **p** is that the first is voiced and the second is voiceless. You will see later what this means.

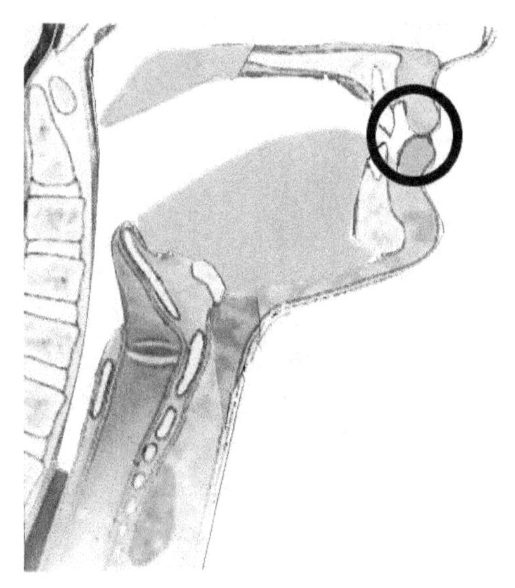

■ LABIODENTAL

LABIODENTAL sounds are formed with the lower lip and the upper teeth. **F** and **v** in English are labiodental sounds.

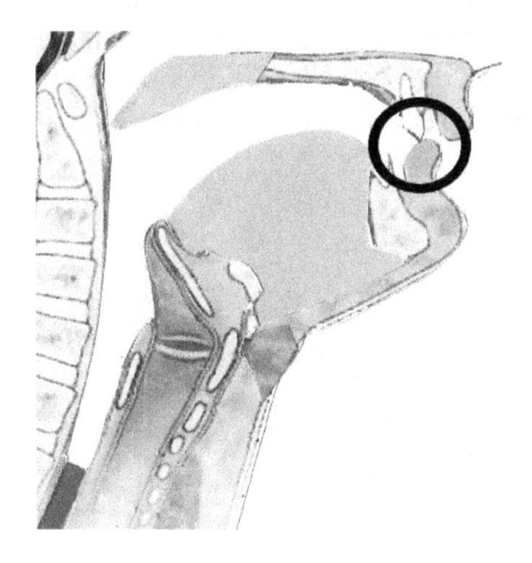

■ DENTAL

In Spanish, we also have **DENTAL** consonants, **t** and **d,** that are formed with the tip of the tongue and the back of the upper incisors.

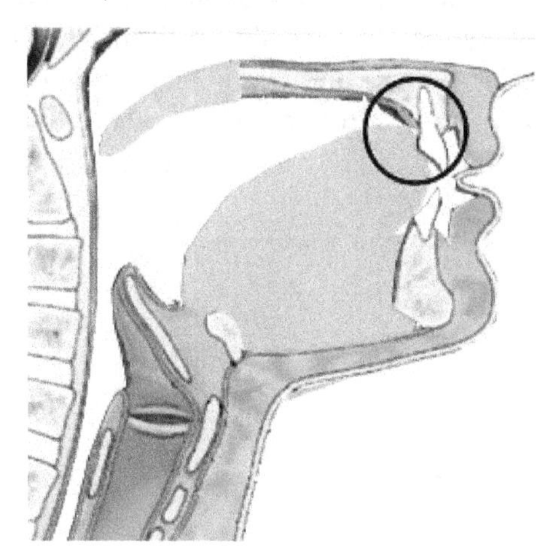

Attention! In English, **t** and **d** are alveolar sounds (see below).

INTERDENTAL

INTERDENTAL sounds are produced with the tip of the tongue between the upper and lower teeth. In English, there are two (2): **th** in `bath` and `bathe`. The symbol for the first sound is [θ] and for the second [ð]. In most of Spain, **z** and **c** (before **e** and **i**) are also interdental. At the end of words, **d** can also be pronounced [θ] in some places, especially in Castille, for example in Madrid [ma.'driθ].

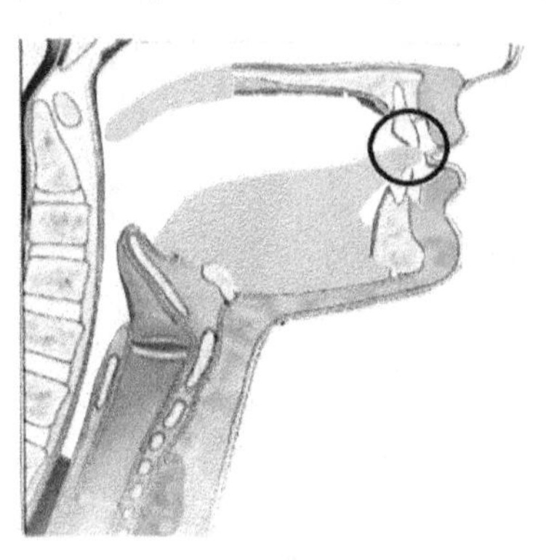

ALVEOLAR

Right behind the upper teeth is the **ALVEOLAR RIDGE**. Explore the inside of your mouth with your tongue and you will feel that behind the alveolar ridge, the palate rises almost vertically. Consonants that are formed with the tongue and the alveolar ridge are consequently called **ALVEOLAR** sounds. In English, **s, z, t, n, l** and **d** are alveolar sounds: `see, zebra, tin, now, low, din.`

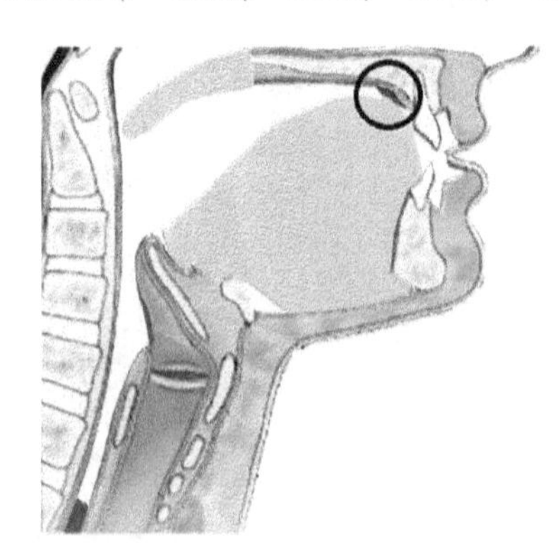

■ PALATAL

PALATAL sounds are formed with the back of the tongue and the hard palate without touching each other. In English, the sounds **sh** in `ash` and **s** in `pleasure` are palatal consonants.

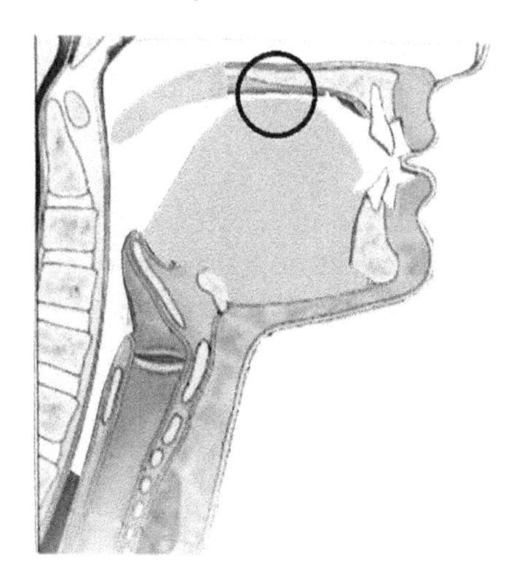

■ VELAR

VELAR consonants **are** articulated with the back of the tongue and the soft palate. The **k** in `kit`, g in `go`, and **ng** in `king` are velar consonants.

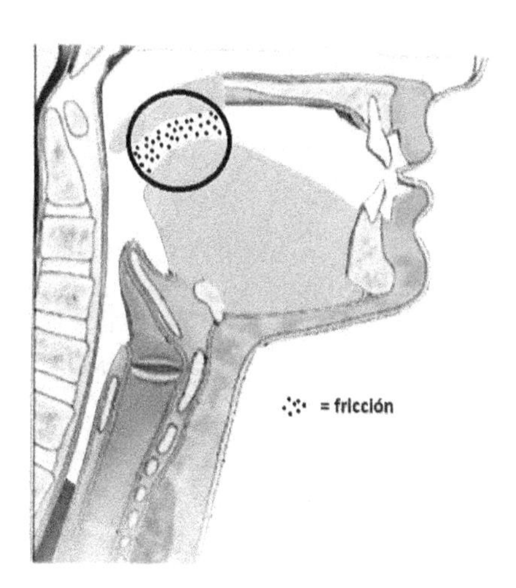

UVULAR

Uvular consonants are formed with the back of the tongue and the uvula. This place of articulation is used in some Spanish dialects, for example the use of [χ] for the /x/ sound in words such as **paja** and **mujer** in the center and north of Spain, and the use of [ʁ] for the /r/ sound in words such as **rasgo** and **perro** in some parts of Puerto Rico.

GLOTTAL

A GLOTTAL sound is produced by the obstruction of the air flow through the GLOTTIS. The English h, for example, is **GLOTTAL**.

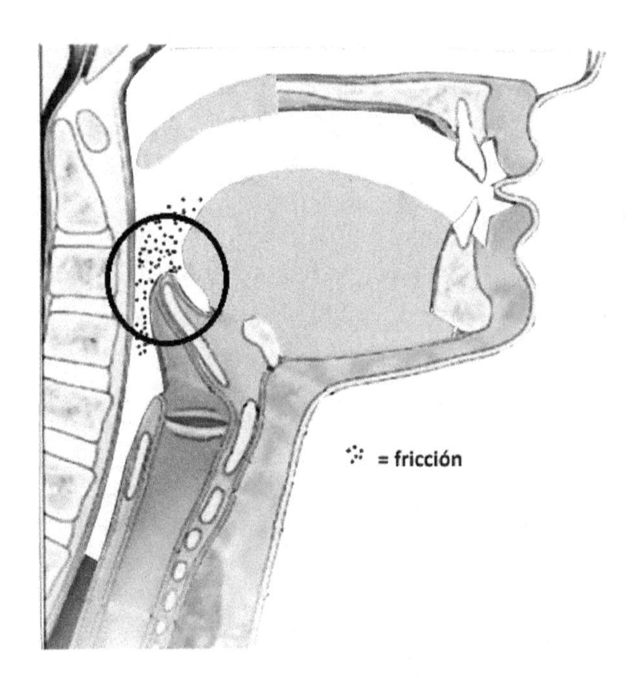

Manner of articulation

The second thing you need to know is HOW consonants are produced, or their **MANNER OF ARTICULATION** (Span. **MODO DE ARTICULACIÓN**). First, we establish if a consonant is nasal or oral, this is if the air leaves the mouth or the nose.

NASAL

NASAL consonants are produced when the velum, or soft palate, is lowered. This allows a large portion of air to pass through the nasal cavity. At the same time, the air is blocked with the tongue and the lips so that it must exit through the nose.

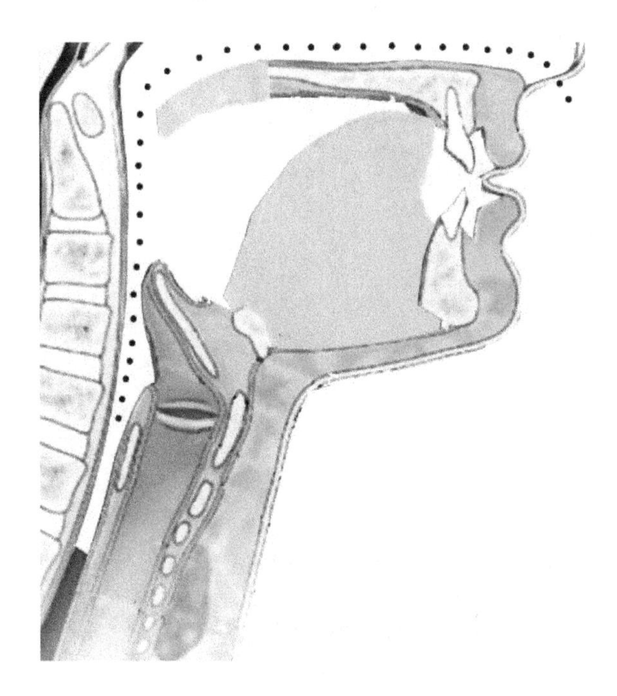

The **m** in `more`, the **n** in `nor` and the **ng** in `sing` are nasal consonants. In Spanish, there are three (3) nasal phonemes, /m/, /n/ and /ɲ/, and a series of allophones. All the other consonants are **ORAL** consonants.

■ ORAL

Oral sounds are produced when the soft palate is in an elevated position and blocks the passage of air through the nose into the nasal cavity. The air must leave through the oral cavity and the mouth. Most consonants in Spanish are oral.

Within the oral consonants we further distinguish the way in which the flow of air is obstructed in the oral cavity. The possibilities are:

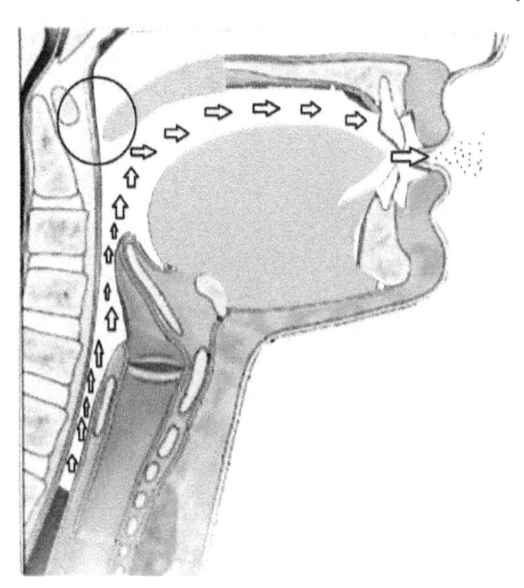

• FRICATIVES

Some consonants are partially obstructed before exiting the mouth, which has the effect that the airflow experiences friction. Consequently, these sounds are called **FRICATIVES**. The **s** in `see`, the **f** in `free` and the **s** in `pleasure` are fricative sounds.

• APPROXIMANTS

When the obstruction is too weak to cause audible friction, we call the sounds **APPROXIMANTS**. Examples are the allophones [β], [ð], and [ɣ] of the phonemes /b/, /d/, /g/.

STOPS

An **STOP** or **PLOSIVE** consonant is a sound in which the airflow is first completely stopped to produce pressure and then released. The **p** in `pin`, the **t** in `tin` and the **k** in `kin` are occlusives. **B** and **g** in `big` and **d** in `din` voiced stops (See below under 'Voicing'). There are quite a few stops in English and Spanish.

AFFRICATES

AFFRICATES are a combination of stops and fricatives. The **ch** in `chin` is an affricate. Essentially two sounds, first a stop followed by a fricative, make up affricates.

LATERALS

LATERALS are sounds that are produced when the tongue obstructs the air flow in the center of the mouth which causes the air to be re-routed on both sides of the tongue and the mouth. An example of a lateral sound in Spanish is the [l].

TAPS, FLAPS and TRILLS

TAPS, **FLAPS** and **TRILLS** (Span. **VIBRANTES SENCILLAS Y MÚLTIPLES**) are produced by vibration or rapid closure, one or several times, of the front of the tongue against the alveolar ridge. The sound **[ɾ]** in **caro** is a simple tap (or flap) and the sound **[r]** in **carro** is a trill. The **r** in English is neither of these. (You will see later in this book that there is another English sound that is similar to the Spanish single tap (or flap) **[ɾ]**.)

Voicing

The third characteristic of a consonant that you must know is whether it is **VOICED** or **VOICELESS** (Span. **SORDA** or **SONORA**). If you put your finger on your VOICE BOX (Span. **LARINGE**) when you articulate [m] or [g], you will feel the vibrations of your vocal cords because those two sounds are voiced. When you produce the sound of **f** or **sh**, with your fingers in the same place, you will not feel any vibration, because those sounds are unvoiced. The **p** of `pin` is the unvoiced counterpart of the voiced **b** in `bin`. The **s** of `phase` is the voiced equivalent of the unvoiced **c** in `face`.

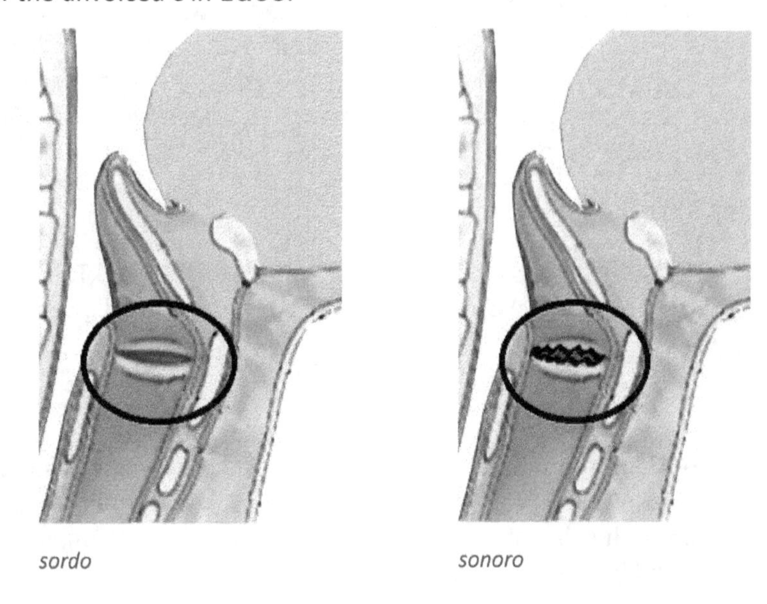

sordo *sonoro*

Once you know these three (3) reference points, you can describe virtually any consonant, whether it exists in English or not, and the person you describe it to –knowing the same three concepts– should be able to produce it. So, if you say that the **g** in **ganar** in Spanish is a "voiced velar stop", your friend should be able to reproduce it. If your French or German friend can't seem to pronounce the initial **th** of `think` (that sound doesn't exist in French and German), he or she may say `sink`, fink or `zinc` instead, all you need to do is say: "No, no, don't you see? It's an unvoiced interdental fricative!" And that should do the trick, but only if that person knows these phonetic definitions. The problem is that the sound is new to that person, and old habits are tough to break; new habits are tough to acquire. Bear this in mind if your progress seems slow in this course.

Questions

1. What is the difference between a vowel and a consonant?
2. What are glides?
3. Which are the three characteristics used to describe a consonant?
4. Which is the place of articulation of a bilabial sound?
5. Which is the place of articulation of a labio-dental sound?
6. Which is the place of articulation of a dental sound?
7. Which is the place of articulation of an interdental sound?
8. Which is the place of articulation of an alveolar sound?
9. Which is the place of articulation of a palatal sound?
10. Which is the place of articulation of a velar sound?
11. Which is the place of articulation of a uvular sound?
12. Which is the place of articulation of a glottal sound?
13. How is a fricative produced?
14. What is an approximant?
15. How is a stop produced?
16. How is an affricate sound produced?
17. How is a nasal sound produced?
18. How is a lateral sound produced?
19. How are taps (flaps) and trills produced?
20. What is voicing, and which sounds are voiced and voiceless?

Exercises

1. The vocal apparatus. Fill out the crossword.

Horizontal:

1 The gum-covered ridge of bone behind the teeth in the upper jaw is called the ________________ ridge.

3 The [χ] sound in words such as "paja" and "mujer" in the center and north of Spain is an __________________ sound.

6 The sound [p] en "playa" is formed with both ____________.

8 Labiodental sounds are formed with the ____________ lip and the upper teeth.

9 The air exits though the _______________ when we pronounce nasal consonants.

10 The [d] in "dar" is a dental consonant. The tip of the tongue touches the upper _____________.

Vertical:

2 When you feel a vibration of the _______________ cords when you pronounce a consonant such as [b] it is voiced.

3 A labio-dental sound is made with the lower lip and the _____________ teeth.

4 The voiced box is also called _________________.

5 The ____________ is the roof of the mouth.

7 The soft palate is also called the ______________.

11 Interdental sounds, for example the [θ] sound in Spain, are produced with the _______________of the tongue between the upper and lower teeth.

2. Terminology to describe consonants. Fill in the blanks:

a A (1) ___________ is a sound that comes out of the mouth without any obstruction.
b A (2) _____________ is a sound that has some impediment that squeezes, stops or reroutes the sound before it leaves the mouth.
c The (3)___________ is the spot in the mouth where the (4)___________ takes place.
d The (5)___________ is how a sound is articulated;
e The (6) ___________ of the (7) ___________ cords or the lack of it determines if a consonant is voiced or voiceless.
f A consonant is (8) ___________ when there is a vibration of the vocal cords.
g A consonant is (9) ___________ when there is NO vibration of the vocal cords.
h Voicing: [p] is a (10)___________ sound.
i Voicing: [s] is a (11)___________ sound.
j Voicing: [b] is a (12)___________ sound.

3. Place and manner of articulation. Fill out the crossword.

Horizontal:

2 A consonant that is articulated with the front of the tongue and the alveolar ridge.

5 A consonant with obstruction too weak to cause audible friction.

6 A consonant that is pronounced with the tip of the tongue between the teeth.

7 A consonant where the air is obstructed in the center of the mouth and released on both sides of the tongue/ mouth.

8 When the airflow exits through the nose, we have a __________ consonant.

11 A consonant that combines a complete closure and friction is called _________.

13 When the air is obstructed with both lips, we have a ___________ consonant.

16 Sounds produced without vibration of the vocal cords are ________.

17 Several vibrations of the tongue are called _______.

18 The [h] in English is a __________ sound.

19 A consonant articulated with the velum and the back of the tongue is ________.

Vertical:

1 A single vibration of the tongue is called _________.

3 When the vocal cords vibrate during the production of the sound, it is ________.

4 A consonant produced with the upper teeth and the lower lip is called __________.

9 A sound with a lot of friction is called a ______________.

10 A complete closure or blockage of the air flow produces an _________ consonant.

12 A consonant produced with the hard palate and the tongue is called ___________.

14 A ____________ consonant is produced with the uvula.

15 A consonant where the tip of the tongue touches the back of the front teeth is called ____________.

7
Voiceless stops (plosives) /p/, /t/, /k/

In this chapter, we will describe the phonemes or families of sounds /p/, /t/ and /k/. (The **PHONEME** concept has been explained in Chapter 1.)

The phonemes /p/, /t/ and /k/ share two essential characteristics: all are plosives and voiceless. What sets them apart is the place of articulation. The voicing distinguishes them from the voiced phonemes /b/, /d/ and /g/.

As you can see below, in Spanish, each phoneme has just one member or **ALLOPHONE**. These sounds are pronounced the same way in every allowable phonetic environment. Still, you may need some practice to master the correct pronunciation of [p], [t] and [k] in Spanish because of interference with English where the phonemes have two allophones. Below are the phonemes and allophones in Spanish:

The phoneme /p/

[p] **VOICELESS BILABIAL STOP** (UNASPIRATED)

in all contexts: **pensar [pen.'sar], presa ['pre.sa], esperar [es.pe.'rar], aplauso [a.'plaw.so], capa ['ka.pa]**, etc.

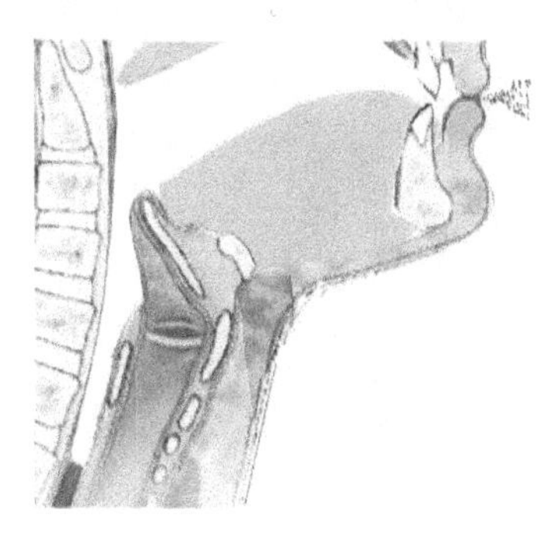

The phoneme /t/

[t] **VOICELESS DENTAL STOP** (UNASPIRATED)

in all contexts: **tal ['tal], estrella [es.'tre.ʝa], hasta ['as.ta], trigo ['tri.ɣo], matar [ma.'taɾ]**, etc.

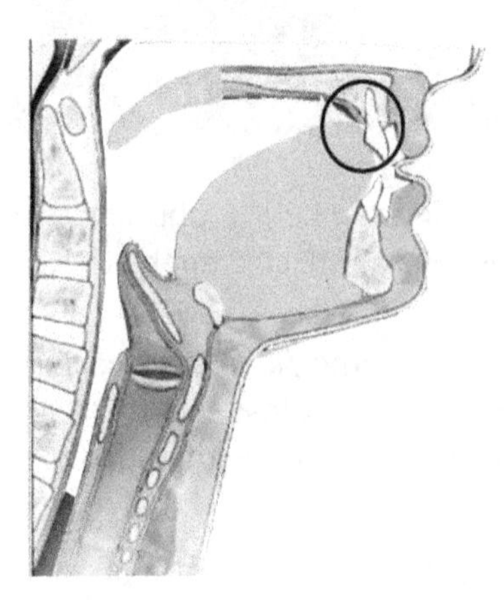

The phoneme /k/

[k] **VOICELESS VELAR STOP** (UNASPIRATED)

in all contexts: **calor [ka.'loɾ], asco ['as.ko], accidente [ak.si.'den̪.te], aquí [a.'ki], clave ['kla.βe], bikini [bi.'ki.ni]**, etc.

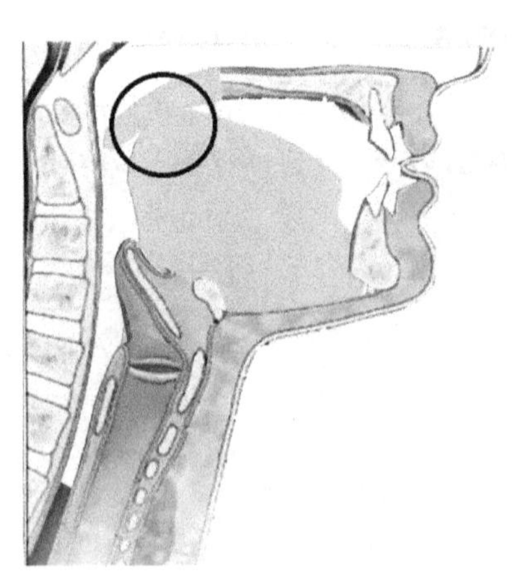

The phonemes /p/, /t/, /k/ in English

A look at the English phonemes shows the contexts where the English pronunciation could interfere with your pronunciation in Spanish.

/p/

[pʰ] **VOICELESS BILABIAL STOP** (ASPIRATED)
at the beginning of words or stressed syllables: pit [ˈpʰɪt], peck [ˈpʰɛk], impeccable [ɪm.ˈpʰɛ.kə.bəl]

[p] **VOICELESS BILABIAL STOP** (UNASPIRATED)
in all other contexts: spit [ˈspɪt], speck [ˈspɛk], lap [ˈlæp], aspiration [æ.spə.ˈɹeɪ.ʃən], caps [ˈkʰæps]

/t/

[tʰ] **VOICELESS ALVEOLAR STOP** (ASPIRATED)
at the beginning of words or stressed syllables: tick [ˈtʰɪk], tall [ˈtʰɔl], attract [ə.ˈtɹækt]

[ɾ] **VOICED SINGLE ALVEOLAR FLAP**
between vowels, written **t** or **tt:** later [ˈleɪ.ɾɚ], better [ˈbɛ.ɾɚ], I gotta go [eɪ.ˈgɑ. ɾə.ˈgoʊ], get up [ˈgɛ.ˈɾʌp], get outta bed [ˈgɛ.ˈɾaʊ.ɾə.ˈbɛd]

[t] **VOICELESS ALVEOLAR STOP** (UNASPIRATED)
in all other contexts: stick [ˈstɪk], stall [ˈstɔl], heat [ˈhit], hats [ˈhæts], lasting [ˈlæ.stɪŋ]

/k/

[kʰ] **VOICELESS VELAR STOP** (ASPIRATED)
at the beginning of words or stressed syllables: cat [ˈkʰæt], kin [ˈkʰɪn], incredible [ɪŋ.ˈkʰɹɛ.ɾə.bəl]

[k] **VOICELESS VELAR STOP** (UNASPIRATED)
in all other contexts: skin [ˈskɪn], track [ˈtɹæk], lacks [ˈlæks], asking [ˈæ.skɪŋ]

You can easily see the interference trap. If you apply the English phonotactics to Spanish, **p, t, k** at the beginning of words and stressed syllables will be aspirated: instead of **para** ['pa.ra] you will say ['pʰa.ra], instead of **tío** ['ti.o] you will say ['tʰi.o], and instead of **caro** ['ka.ro] you will say ['kʰa.ro]. You can feel if you aspirate [p], [t], [k], when you put your hand or a candle in front of your mouth.

The simple flap sound [ɾ] is not an allophone of /t/ in Spanish as can be seen in the minimal pairs **rato** ['ra.to] vs. **raro** ['ra.ro].

Remember also that the **t** in Spanish is dental, and not alveolar as in English. This means that it is produced with the front of the tongue and the back of the upper teeth.

Let's practice!

In the following we will provide you some methods to help you overcome these interference problems. Avoiding aspiration isn't as hard as it might seem. English `pit`, `tick` and `cab` have aspirated sounds in initial position, but if you change them into words with initial **s**, they are never aspirated, not even in English: `spit`, `stick` and `scab`. So, if you do exercises in Spanish where the **ptk** are not in initial position and gradually work around to where they are, you can fool your vocal tract into producing the Spanish sounds correctly. For example, if you link the name **Oscar** together many times and change it into **caros**, the [k] sound won't be aspirated:

Example:	**Oscar**
Say:	**OscarOscarOscarOscarOscarOscar**

and after a while, move the beginning of the word to the second syllable: **caroscaroscaroscaroscaroscaros**, maintaining the pronunciation of the **c** of **caros** without aspiration in **Oscar**.

You can practice the pronunciation of unaspirated initial **t** and **p** also with the words **costar/ tarcos** and **aspar/ paras**.

Another trick to avoid aspiration is pronouncing initial **ptk** as if they were **bdg** because these voiced sounds don't have aspiration. Start with initial **bdg** and then make them voiceless:

Example: **Basta**

Repeat **basta** ten (10) times or more and then change it to **pasta** (unaspirated and voiceless). There are similar exercises at the end of this chapter.

Another issue with the **t** in Spanish is that it is dental and not alveolar as in English. This means that it is formed with the front of the tongue pressing against the back of the upper teeth. There is no easy fix for this problem. It simply requires practice to remember to touch the tongue to the back of the teeth instead of the alveolar ridge.

Word final consonants are the least stable sounds in Spanish, which resulted in the loss of many of them during the evolution from Latin to Castilian. Exceptions are final **–s** and **–n**. Words that in modern Spanish end in consonants other than **–s** and **–n**, for example **final** and **dolor**, lost a final **–e,** as you can still see in Italian, for example, where we have `finale` and `dolore`. Others are loan words from foreign languages. All the words ending in [p], [t], [k] in modern Spanish were adapted with the same or similar spelling as other languages, for example **schop**, **ketchup**, **hándicap**, **ballet**, **cabaret**, **carnet**, **cenit**, **chalet**, **Internet**, **robot**, **sabbat**, **ticket**, **zenit**, **anorak**, **kayak**, **rock**, **bistec**, **cómic**, **crac**, **picnic**, etc. The most common are written the way they are pronounced in Spanish, without the final consonant, and can be found in the Dictionary of the Spanish Language Academy, for example: **bisté**, **cabaré**, **carné**, **chalé**, **tique.**

Exercises

The phoneme /p/

1. **In English, p after s is unaspirated, unless it starts a stressed syllable. Repeat the following list of words where the p starts an unstressed syllable.**

caspa	obispos	esperar
esperar	áspero	español
obispo	desesperado	espiral
áspero	diáspora	hospital
césped	disparar	perspicaz
chispas	disponer	próspero
huésped	disputar	

2. **Now repeat the following list of words that start with p preceded by the articles los and las. First, pronounce them as if the article and the noun together were a word and then add a short pause between the s and the p maintaining the unaspirated [p].**

lospedazos	los pedazos	lospeligros	los peligros
laspajadas	las pajadas	laspelículas	las películas
lospacientes	los pacientes	lospilotos	los pilotos
lospadrinos	los padrinos	lospimientos	los pimientos
laspaellas	las paellas	laspiñatas	las piñatas
lospaisajes	los paisajes	lospoderes	los poderes
laspalabras	las palabras	lospoemas	los poemas
lospeinados	los peinados	lospolicías	los policías
laspreguntas	las preguntas	lospulmones	los pulmones

3. **A b at the beginning of a word in English is always unaspirated. The purpose of this exercise is to "trick" your vocal tract. First, repeat the word in the first column several times (babel/babel/babel...) and then the word in the second column (papel/papel/papel...). Remember to avoid the aspiration of [p] as if it were [b].**

baja	paja	banda	panda
bajada	pajada	baño	paño
bala	pala	bar	par

basa	pasa	boca	poca
basto	pasto	bollo	pollo
bata	pata	bomba	pompa
beca	peca	borra	porra
besar	pesar	bote	pote
beso	peso		

4. Now read the following sayings aloud.

1 Al buen pagador no le duelen prendas.

2 La perdiz por el pico se pierde.

3 Palos porque bogas, palos porque no bogas.

4 Perdiendo aprendí: más vale lo que aprendí que lo que perdí.

5 El que mucho abarca poco aprieta.

6 El que compra barato, compra a cada rato.

5. Read the following tongue twisters.

Debajo de aquella pequeña peña,
hay otra peña más pequeña
que la peña pequeña,
que había encima
de la peña más pequeña.

The phoneme /t/

6. After an s, [t] is unaspirated in English, unless it begins a stressed syllable. Repeat the list of words below where the t begins an unstressed syllable:

esta	estadística	estación	estatura
estimular	estudiar	castellano	castigar
costa	destacar	destilería	distinción
fiesta	festival	gasto	gusto
hasta	justo	lástima	místico

7. **Now repeat the pairs of words that start with t but that are preceded by the articles los and las. First, pronounce them as if the article and the noun together were a word and then make a little pause between the s and the t maintaining the unaspirated [t].**

lostambores	los tambores	lostobillos	los tobillos
lostabacos	los tabacos	lostoledanos	lostoledanos
lostaburetes	los taburetes	lostomates	los tomates
lostalentos	los talentos	lastonterías	las tonterías
losteatros	los teatros	lastormentas	las tormentas
lostetclados	los teclados	losturistas	los turistas
lostejidos	los tejidos	lostucanes	los tucanes
losteléfonos	los teléfonos	lasturbinas	las turbinas
lostemores	los temores	losturrones	los turrones
las tenazas	las tenazas		

8. **A d at the beginning of a word in English is never aspirated. First, repeat several times the word in the first column (dejado/dejado/dejado ...) and then the word in the second column (tejado/tejado/tejado ...). Remember to avoid the aspiration of the [t] as if it were a [d].**

dan	tan	deja	teja	doce	tose
dango	tango	déjalo	téjalo	Dora	tora
dardo	tardo	deje	teje	domar	tomar
data	tata	dejo	tejo	danto	tanto
daza	taza	dele	tele	dos	tos
debajo	te bajo	denso	tenso	duna	tuna
debate	te bate	día	tía		

9. **A t before u is often pronounced like ch, for example in `chin` or sh in `shin` in English. In Spanish, however, a t is always dental. Read the following pairs of words in English and Spanish. (They don't always have the same meaning.)**

actual	actual	lecturer	lectura
adventure	aventura	mutual	mutuo
conceptual	conceptual	natural	natural
cultural	cultural	overture	obertura
eventual	eventual	ritual	ritual
habitual	habitual	virtual	virtual
intellectual	intelectual	textual	textual

10. Now read the following sayings aloud.

A los tontos no les dura el dinero.
Tanto monta, monta tanto.
Tanto tienes, tanto vales; nada tienes, nada vales.
El que temprano se moja, tiempo tiene de secarse.

The phoneme /k/

11. After an s, [k] is unaspirated in English, unless it begins a stressed syllable. Repeat the list of words below where the k begins an unstressed syllable:

asco	escalar	escalera	escasez
buscador	búsqueda	máscara	músculo
pescador	emboscada	mayúscula	minúscula
rascacielos	casco	exquisito	fresco
bosque	morisco	mariscos	quiosco

12. Now repeat the following list of words that start with k preceded by the articles los and las. First, pronounce them as if the article and the noun together were a word and then make a little pause between the s and the c/k/qu maintaining the unaspirated [k].

loscamarones	los camarones
losqueridos	los queridos
losquetzales	los quetzales
loskilómetros	los kilómetros
losquioscos	los quioscos
lascamisas	las camisas
loscaimanes	los caimanes
loscaballos	los caballos
lascabañas	las cabañas
loscabellos	los cabellos
lascabezas	las cabezas
lascabinas	las cabinas

loscobijos	los cobijos
loscocineros	los cocineros
loscocodrilos	los cocodrilos
loscochinos	los cochinos
loscuadernos	los cuadernos
loscubiertos	los cubiertos
loscuchillos	los cuchillos
lasculebras	las culebras

13. A g at the beginning of a word is always unaspirated. First, repeat several times the word in the first column (galo/galo/galo ...), then repeat the word in the second column several times (calo/calo/calo ...) concentrating on the unaspirated [g] sound when you produce [k].

galo	calo	gata	cata
gacha	cacha	gato	cato
gacho	cacho	gaucho	caucho
gala	cala	gayo	cayo
gallo	callo	godo	codo
gama	cama	gola	cola
gano	cano	goda	coda
gasa	casa	goma	coma
gasta	casta	gorra	corra
gasto	casto	gorro	corro

14. Now read the following sayings aloud.

Adonde el corazón se inclina, el pie camina.

A quien Dios quiere para sí, poco tiempo lo tiene aquí.

Cortesía de boca mucho consigue y nada cuesta.

De cuerdo y loco todos tenemos un poco.

El casado casa quiere.

En casa de carpintero, puerta de cuero.

Mal que no tiene cura, quererlo curar es locura.

El que tiene boca se equivoca.

Final exercise

15. The following sentences were taken from various newspaper articles. Read them aloud and pay attention to the pronunciation of /p, t , k/ in different phonetic environments.

1 Le faltó sorpresa y se quedó a mitad de camino entre la propuesta y la actitud.

2 El fiscal reconstruyó las últimas horas de Axel, desde que intentó escaparse de la casilla donde estaba cautivo.

3 Los policías antisecuestros cordobeses tenían ubicado el lugar y se disponían a actuar.

4 El gobierno inició conversaciones para alcanzar un acuerdo bilateral y se trataría de favorecer la llegada de productos argentinos.

5 Los tres detenidos fueron trasladados en un avión de la gobernación, desde el Aeropuerto Córdoba.

6 Mil quinientos efectivos están destinados a la custodia y no pueden ocuparse del patrullaje callejero.

7 Gaudí fue un referente para Dalí, tanto en su obra como en sus escritos. Lo valora mucho como arquitecto y por su sentimiento católico.

8 La pedrera, el Park Güell y la Sagrada Familia son los ejes centrales del recorrido y en torno a los cuales se estructuran los dibujos, pinturas y documentos.

9 La estructura ideada por el presidente y ejecutada por Jorge Valdano, también en entredicho, ha caído del altar por el peso de problemas futbolísticos y por una actitud de soberbia y exceso de confianza que ha terminado por pasar factura.

8

Voiced stops (plosives) /b/, /d/, /g/, /ɟ/

In this chapter, we will describe the phonemes or families of sounds /b/, /d/ and /g/. (The **PHONEME** concept has been explained in Chapter 1.)

The phonemes /b/, /d/ and /g/ share two essential characteristics: all are voiced and plosive. What sets them apart from each other is their place of articulation. Voicing distinguishes them from the voiceless phonemes /p/, /t/, /k/.

Furthermore, the families /b/, /d/ and /g/ in Spanish have each two members, an occlusive and an approximant variant. This series of phonemes has two sounds that don't exist in English. We will explain how and when they are used so that you can practice them and get accustomed to their usage.

The phoneme /b/

[b] VOICED BILABIAL STOP

absolute initial position, i.e. after a pause: **¡Bueno!** ['bwe.no], **¡Victoria!** [bik.'to.rja]

after nasal sound: **hambre** ['am.bre], **envío** [em.'bi.o], **un burro** [um.'bu.ro], **un vaso** [um.'ba.so], etc.

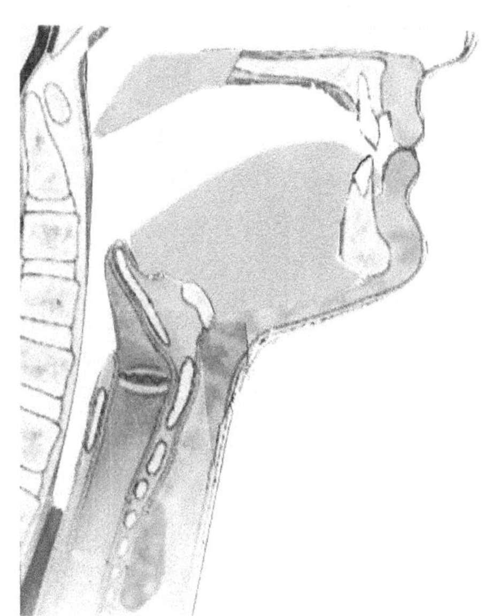

[β] VOICED BILABIAL APPROXIMANT

all other positions: **árbol** ['ar.βol], **calvo** ['kal.βo], **fabuloso** [fa.βu.'lo.so], **llevar** [ɟe.'βar], **fiebre** ['fje.βre], **obligación** [o.βli.ga.'sjon], **alba** ['al.βa], **Cervantes** [ser.'βan.tes], **abstracto** [aβs.'trak.to]

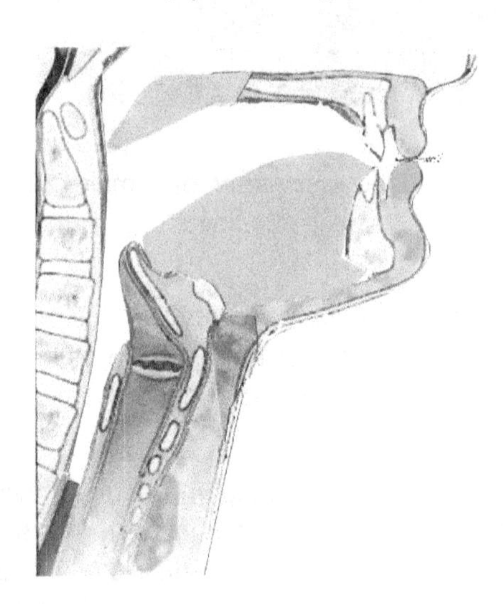

The phoneme /d/

[d] VOICED DENTAL STOP

absolute initial position, i.e. after a pause: **¡Despiértense!** [des.'pjer.ten.se]

after a nasal sound: **andar** [an.'dar], **un diputado** [un.di.pu.'ta.ðo]

after **l**: **caldo** ['kal.do], **aldea** [al.'de.a], **el dorado** [el.do.'ra.ðo]

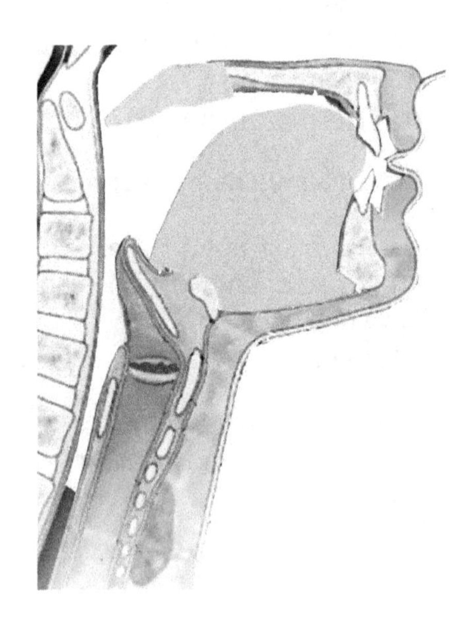

[ð] VOICED DENTAL APPROXIMANT

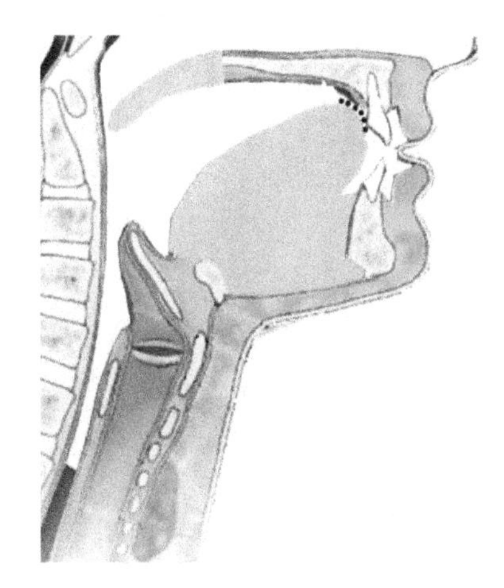

all other positions: **hada** ['a.ða], **odontología** [o.ðon.to.lo.'xi.a], **padre** ['pa.ðre], **cuadro** ['kwa.ðro], **ardiente** [ar.'ðjen.te], **desde** ['des.ðe], **calidad** [ka.li.'ðað]

The phoneme /g/

[g] VOICED VELAR STOP

absolute initial position, i.e. after pause: **¡gracias a Dios!** ['gra.sja.sa.'ðjos] **gané la lotería.** [ga.'ne.la.lo.te.'ri.a]

after nasal sound: **un gato** [uŋ.'ga.to], **tengo** ['teŋ.go], **un álbum gracioso** [u.'nal.βum.gra.'sjo.so]

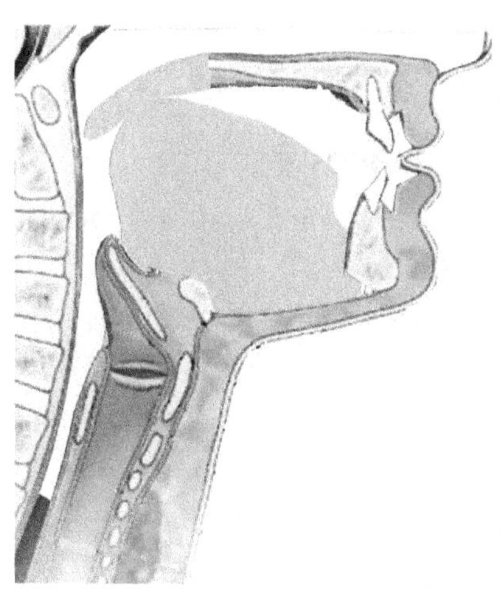

[ɣ] VOICED VELAR APPROXIMANT

all other positions: **vinagre** [bi.'na.ɣre], **órgano** ['or.ɣa.no], **algo** ['al.ɣo], **arguye** [ar.'ɣu.ʝe], **hago** ['a.ɣo]

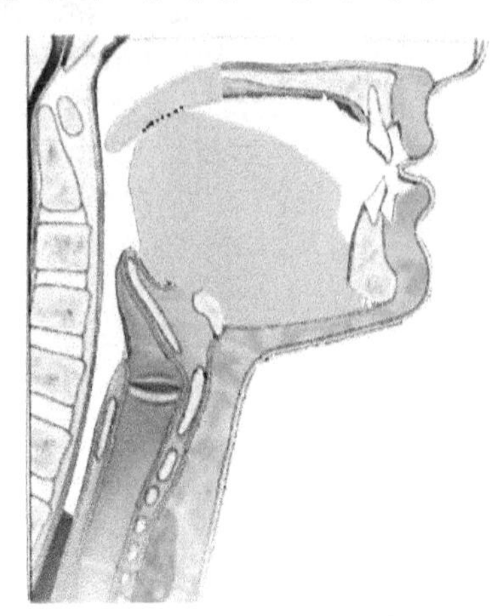

Attention! You already know that the letters **b** and **v** are pronounced the same way and both graphemes represent the phoneme /b/. The **v** is NOT labiodental as in English. (See Chapter 2)

In general, the same phonetic context affects the three phonemes the same way, with the exception of the **/d/**, which remains a stop after **/l/**.

The phoneme /ɟ/

[ɟ] VOICED PALATAL PLOSIVE

absolute initial position, i.e. after a pause:: **llamar** [ɟa.'mar], **yacer** [ɟa.'ser]

after nasal sounds: **cónyuge** ['koŋ.ɟu.ɣe], **inyección** [iŋ.ɟek.'sjon], conllevar [koŋ.ɟe.'βar]

after lateral sound: **el yeso** [eʎ.'ɟe.so], **mil llaves** [miʎ.'ɟa.βes]

[ʝ] VOICED PALATAL FRICATIVE

all other positions: **calle** ['ka.ʝe], **maya** ['ma.ʝa], **leyes** ['le.ʝes], etc.

■ The sound [ʝ]

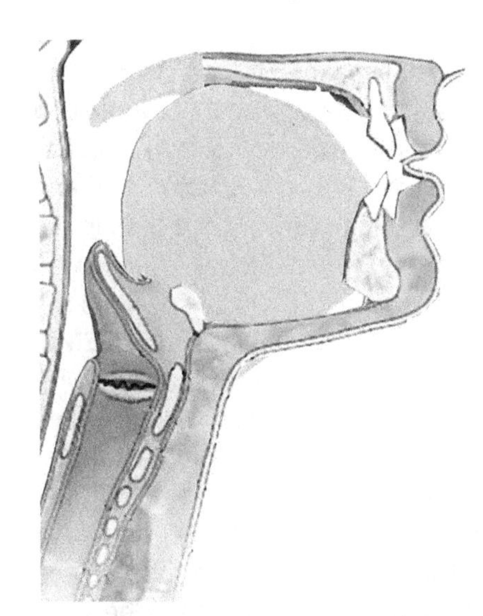

There is so much variation in the pronunciation of the letters **ll** and **y** that there is a lack of agreement about whether the phoneme associated with the corresponding sounds is the palatal stop /ɟ/, or the palatal fricative /ʝ/ (or even a combination of both, the affricate /ɟʝ/). Without further complicating the matter, we follow Hualde (2005) and Morgan (2010), in classifying /ɟ/ as the phoneme with the allophones [ɟ] and [ʝ]. In addition to representing the distribution of these sounds well, it is also an elegant solution to the problem of the allophones: the environments where the stop variant is used are the same in which the stop variant of /d/ is used: absolute initial position, after nasals, and after /l/. Still, we recognize that even within this explanation, there is a lot of variation in the production of these sounds.

The allophone [ɟ] is a **voiced central palatal stop.** It is written **ll** and **y**, for example in the words **calle** and **hoyo**. It is like the **j** at the beginning of English words such as `jog,` but not identical.

The allophone [ʝ] is a **voiced central palatal fricative** sound. It is also written **ll** and **y**, for example in the words **llama** and **inyección**. It is like the **y** in the English word `yes,` but not identical. In Spanish, this sound is produced with more tension and friction than in English. There are also many dialectal variations of this sound.

The consonantal sound [ʝ] is different from the semivowel [j] in the diphthongs **ie, ei, ia, ai, io, oi**, in words such as **hielo**, **aceite**, **aire**, **hacia**, **ocio**, **boina**, etc. and in triphthongs, for example in **miau**, because the amount of friction is much greater for [ʝ]. (See Chapters 1 and 5.)

The majority of Spanish speakers, especially in the Americas, does not distinguish between **ll** and **y** and pronounce both letters the same way. This phenomenon is called **YEÍSMO**. For yeísta speakers, **halla** and **haya** sound alike.

There is, however, a small number of speakers, for example in the northwestern part of the Iberic Peninsula, in Castilla León, La Rioja and Cantabria, but also in some regions of Latin America, especially in Paraguay and the Andes, that still distinguish the pronunciation of **ll** and **y**, and who articulate **ll** as a **voiced lateral palatal** sound, which is like a combination of the two sounds [l] and [ʝ], and which is represented in the phonetic transcription with the symbol [ʎ]. These speakers say ['ka.ʎe] instead of ['ka.ʝe]. Linguists call this pronunciation **LLEÍSMO**. Lleísta speakers pronounce pairs of words spelled with **ll** and **y**, with different meanings, for example **callo** ['ka.ʎo] and **cayo** ['ka.ʝo], **desmallar** [des.ma.'ʎaɾ] and **desmayar** [des.ma.'ʝaɾ], **malla** ['ma.ʎa] and **maya** ['ma.ʝa], **mallo** ['ma.ʎo] and **mayo** ['ma.ʝo], **pollo** ['po.ʎo] and **poyo** ['po.ʝo], **rallo** ['ra.ʎo] and **rayo** ['ra.ʝo], **valla** ['ba.ʎa] and **vaya** ['ba.ʝa], etc. differently from each other. But because in most of the Spanish speaking world these words sound alike, they have become homophones (= words with the same pronunciation but different meanings) and listeners have to use the context to disambiguate them.

Within the yeísta area there is a lot of geographic and sociocultural variation of **ll** and **y**, which can be heard especially in the Río de la Plata region, where we find the following pronunciations of the word **yo**:

[ʒ]	**yo** [ʒo]	voiced palatal fricative
[ɟ]	**yo** [ɟo]	voiced palatal stop
[ʃ]	**yo** [ʃo]	voiceless palatal fricative

These sounds are not distinctive, which means there aren't any words in Spanish with different meanings that are only distinguished by how the [ʝ] sound is pronounced.

You can find more information about this topic in the chapter about variation.

There are some loan words from Italian and English that are written with g but that are pronounced [ʝ] and not [x] such as the majority of Spanish words: gigolo = [ʝi.ɣo.'lo] (and not *[xi.ɣo.'lo]), gentleman = ['ʝen̪.tel.man] (and not ['xen̪.tel.man]).

The phonemes and allophones in English

/b/

[b] VOICED BILABIAL STOP

in any position: bless ['blɛs], **fabulous** ['fæ.bju.ləs], gab ['gæb], cabriolet [kæ.bɹi.oʊ.'leɪ], obliterate [ə.'blɪ.ɾ ɚ.ɹeɪt]

/d/

[d] VOICED ALVEOLAR STOP

in any position, except between vowels: dear ['diɹ], hard ['hɑɹd], adrift [ə.'dɹɪft]

[ɾ] SIMPLE ALVEOLAR TAP (OR FLAP)

between vowels: adage ['æ.ɾədʒ], ladder ['læ.ɾɚ], I've had it! ['eɪv.'hæ.'ɾɪt]

/g/

[g] VOICED VELAR STOP

in any position: go ['goʊ], bag ['bæg], agriculture ['æ.gɹə.kʌl.tʃɚ], argon ['ɑɹ.gɑn], sagging ['sæ.gɪŋ]

Let's practice

[b] and [β]

In English, the letters **b** and **v** are NOT pronounced the same way. The letter **b** is always bilabial, and the **v** is always labiodental (formed with the upper teeth and the lower lip).

Because in English, there is only a stop [b] and not an approximant [β], you will need to get used not to closing your lips completely when you see a **b** or **v** in Spanish, except at the beginning of phrases and after nasal sounds, and not using your upper teeth, only your lips.

One way to practice the [β] sound is in the series of words: **alaba - acaba - araba - ataba**, paying attention to not closing your lips completely.

Another possibility is to use a mirror to make sure the lips are not closed completely when you pronounce the [β] sound.

Still another way to practice is by holding a sheet of paper or cardboard between your open lips. First, touch the paper with your two lips when you pronounce **b**, and then do the same without touching the paper. The first one would be a stop and the second one an approximant pronunciation.

Finally, imagine that you want to blow out a candle. Try to do that several times. Now, do the same while pronouncing a **b** in words such as **alaba - acaba - araba - ataba** and try to blow out less and less air, but keeping your lips in the same position in which they were while blowing out the candle.

The pronunciation of the [β] sound is also similar to the [w] sound, the allophone of the phoneme /u/ in the diphthongs [wi], [we], [wo] and [wa], that is also similar to the English [w] in `win`, for example in the words **cuidado**, **cuello**, **cuota**, **cuando**. Observe the position of your lips when you pronounce the [w] sound in these words. Now, say **cuando** and right after that **alabando - acabando - caballo - contrabando - zarabando.** Keep your lips in the same position where they were when you said [wa] in **cuando**. Now do the same with **cuidado** followed by **cabida - debido - prohibido - subido**; followed by - **cabello - caribello - abellota**; **cuota** followed by **alcabota - limpiabotas - lustrabotas - rebotado - sacabotas - sabotaje - tirabotas**.

Many words that are written with a **v** in other languages, are also written with a **v** in Spanish: **divino**, **bovino**, **ovino**, etc. Try to pronounce the **v** in these words with both lips and avoid touching the lower lip with the upper teeth.

In informal speech, the **b** sound in the group –**bs**– at the end of syllables can be so week that it almost disappears, for example **abstraer** = [as.tra'er], **obstáculo** = [o.'sta.ku.lo, **subscribir** = [sus.kri.βir], etc. In some words, the reduction is so frequent, that there are parallel spellings with or without **b**. The spelling without the **b** is preferred today: subscribir = **suscribir**, substancia = **sustancia**, obscuro = **oscuro**, etc.

■ [d] and [ð]

In English, there is a sound that is very similar to the Spanish voiced dental approximant. Both use the transcription symbol [ð]. In English it is the sound of the **th** in `leather` or `bathe`. A good method for practicing the Spanish [ð] sound is to pronounce final **d** first as if it were the **th** in `bathe`, and then to reduce the friction, withdraw the tongue slightly and avoid touching the upper teeth. Practice this with the words: **actitud, altitud, certitud, exactitud, juventud, latitud, multitud, amistad, dificultad, facultad, lealtad, libertad, pubertad, tempestad, voluntad**, etc. Note that in Spanish the approximant [ð] occurs at the end of words, but that [β] and [ɣ] are nonexistent in this position.

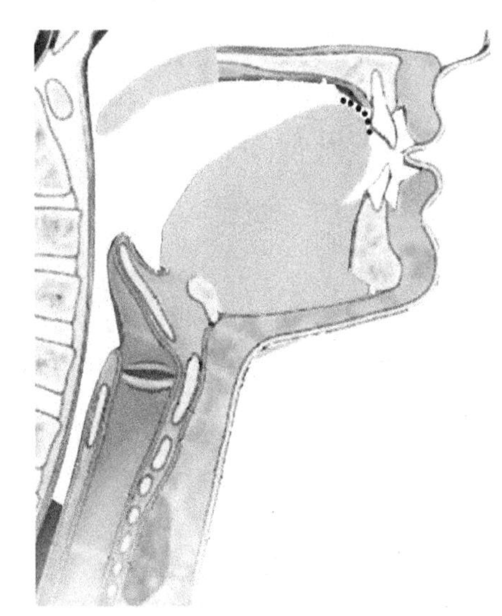

The same tapping or flapping sound [ɾ] of **t** and **tt** between vowels in English also affects **d** or **dd**. In English, [d] and [t] are both alveolar. However, in certain contexts, in English, **d** or **dd** are pronounced like the simple alveolar tap/ flap [ɾ], such as in `lady, ladder, bladder, bedding, edit`, etc. The [ɾ] sound also exists in Spanish, but not as an allophone of the /d/, rather as one of the allophones associated with the /ɾ/, represented by the grapheme **r**. This can be seen in the pairs **cara** and **cada**, **toro** and **todo**, **moro** and **modo**, etc. , which clearly have different meanings. Therefore, you must try to distinguish the sounds [ɾ], [ð] and [t]. Practice this with the following series of words:

- cata [t] - cara [ɾ]- cada [ð]
- Toto[t] - toro [ɾ]- todo [ð]
- moto [t] - moro [ɾ]- modo [ð]
- peta [t] - pera [ɾ]- peda [ð]
- fato [t] - faro [ɾ]- fado[ð]

■ [g] and [ɣ]

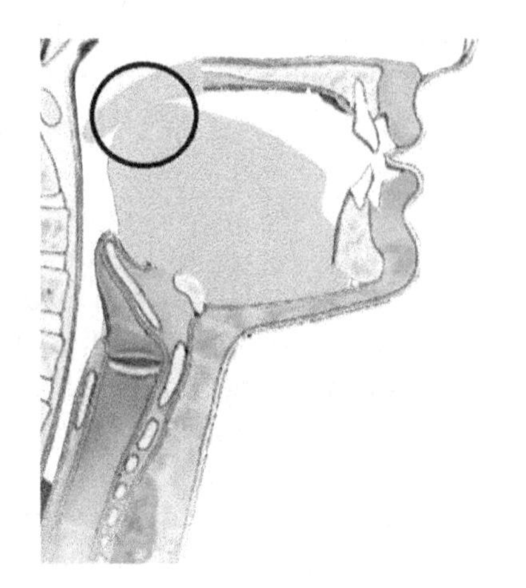

The sound [g]

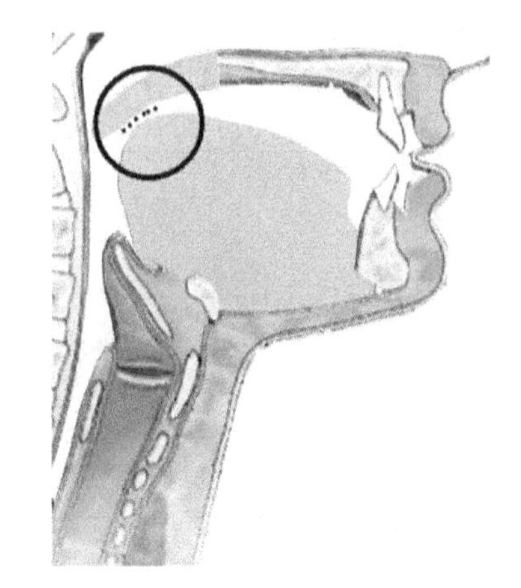

The sound [ɣ]

When you pronounce the [g] in go, you completely close the space between the back of your tongue and the soft palate, or velum. This pronunciation of the [g] is a stop, because of the complete closure. However, in the sentence The sister bought a bi<u>g</u> ba<u>g</u> of su<u>g</u>ar., the underlined **g**s resemble the Spanish approximant [ɣ] because the tongue dorsum and the velum may not create a complete closure, allowing some air to still pass through. In the case of the **g** in big, this is probably because the **b** of the following word, bag, is formed in the front of the mouth, with both lips. To make the transition from a velar to a bilabial sound, there is simply not enough time to complete the closure and the result is a partial closure. Therefore, a useful practice exercise could be the repetition of big bag, big bang, rigband, rigback, twig-basket. Make sure the tongue dorsum does not touch the velum. Now pronounce the Spanish words **bigote**, **bigamia**, **viga**, **vigor**, **vigota** in the same manner. (Remember that **b** and **v** at the beginning of phrases are bilabial stops and that they sound alike.)

■ [ɟ] and [ʝ]

The allophone [ɟ] is a palatal stop, which means that the space between the center body of the tongue and the hard palate is completely closed. In English, this sound doesn't exist, but there are similarities with the sound of the **j** in the English word jog. This is an affricate sound transcribed [dʒ], which does not occur in Spanish. To practice the stop [ɟ], you can start with the name Joe in English. You must control the position of the tongue in the fricative part of the **j**: First, the tongue curves toward the front of the hard palate. Then, it slides back and produces a complete closure with the central part of the hard palate. Repeat this several times and the sound that you produce will be the [ɟ] of **yo**.

You can also practice with the following English and Spanish words: gem - **yema**, jot - **yate**, June - **yunta.**

The allophone [ʝ] is a palatal fricative sound. This means that instead of a complete closure, there is still a narrow space between the tongue and the hard palate, which allows air to be pushed through. This produces friction. Other English and Spanish words that you can use to practice are ajar - **hallar**, danger - **ayer**, edgy - **hoyito**, enjoy - **pollo**, adjust - **ayuda**.

Exercises

The phoneme /b/

1. A v after a pause is always pronounced [b] (voiced bilabial stop).

Victoria	vicaria	víctima	vid
vídeo	vidrio	vidente	vil
villano	voz	vosotros	vocero
vaso	vasco	vascular	vuelo
vuelta	vulgar	vecina	veinte

2. The same goes for v after n. Therefore, the combination nv in con vos sounds like the mb in hombre. Keep this in mind when pronouncing the following words.

circunvolar	con Valerio	con Víctor	convalecer
convencer	conversar	convertir	convivir
convocar	el convento	el envase	el invernadero
el tranvía	en Valencia	en vano	sin vacaciones
enviar	invadir	envejecer	gran ventaja

3. Pronounce the b in the following examples as [β] (voiced bilabial approximant).

débito	debe	doble	debate
debajo	débil	noble	tobillo
tobillo	bobo	cobarde	sabe
Alberto	álbum	abandonar	habitual
habitante	cable	gabinete	cubano

4. Read the following pairs of words and pay attention to the pronunciation of the v in English and Spanish.

cave	cueva
salvation	salvación
cavern	caverna
save	salvar
savage	salvaje
avid	ávido
David	David
my victory	mi victoria
and vice versa	y vice versa

`the position is vacant`	el puesto está vacante
`to be on vacation`	estar de vacaciones
`He is very vicious.`	Él es muy vicioso.
`the vice president`	el vicepresidente
`She is a vegetarian.`	Ella es vegetariana.
`He is very vindictive.`	Él es muy vengativo.

5. Are the letters v and b in the following headlines pronounced [b] or [β]?

1 Detenido en Valencia un presunto etarra que preparaba atentados en Levante para este verano

2 Un perro salva a un vagabundo por un mensaje en una botella

3 Condenado a pagar doscientos veinte euros a un vecino por violar su intimidad al colocar una cámara para vigilar a sus inquilinos

4 El aviso de un vecino conduce a la aprehensión de cuatro mil kilogramos de cocaína en Valencia

The phoneme /d/

6. Pronounce the d in the following words as [d] (voiced dental stop).

dama	Dante	dañar	dar
dato	debajo	decano	decente
dando	candela	andar	aldea
Andalucía	Andrés	Andorra	caldera
balde	molde	onda	banda

7. Pronounce the d in the following examples as a voiced dental approximant [ð].

barbudo	leído	idéntico	comodidad
credibilidad	fidelidad	idealidad	identidad
modalidad	adversidad	solidaridad	productividad
adeudado	estadidad	variedad	acomodado
adecuado	adoptado	graduado	radioactividad

8. Read the following words and decide if the ds should be pronounced [d] or [ð].

fundado	candado	cordialidad	debilidad
densidad	dignidad	diversidad	indignidad
defendido	demanda	difundir	clandestinidad
frondosidad	grandiosidad	profundidad	admisibilidad

The phoneme /g/

9. Read the following words and decide if the gs should be pronounced [g] or [ɣ].

Angola	agave	ingrato	mongol
agobiar	pedagogas	congruente	conglomerado
congratular	sinagoga	agregar	vanguardia
gigante	demagoga	Góngora	segregación
agregar	ganga	Augsburgo	gringo
galápagos	Gregorio	garanta	congregación
pedagoga	gallego	ángulo	griego
segregar	abrigo	agringado	gallegoportugués

10. Read the following sentences taken from different newspapers and pay attention to the pronunciation of the gs in different contexts.

a. El profesor Pérez fue llevado ante el intendente municipal de la ciudad de Buenos Aires, Manuel Güiraldes, quien, poco después, lo designó laringólogo honorario del Teatro Colón que aún no se había inaugurado.

b. José Caminal explicó que en el organigrama del Liceu, como en otros teatros europeos, no figura el cargo de jefe de seguridad.

c. Desde el punto de vista del administrador, un buen organigrama es el que facilita el trabajo y un mal organigrama, el que lo dificulta.

d. ¡Seguro que lo has visto al Maera! El más sangregorda y el más tranquilo en el mundo entero.

e. La empresa, creada por el Grupo Ercrós tras la segregación de Explosivos Río Tinto, podría verse obligada a cerrar definitivamente su segmento de producciones militares.

f. El padre Viganó ha sido un auténtico maestro y guía de la congregación en estos años de renovación y de cambio.

g. En plena campaña para la elección del Parlamento gallego, Fraga reiteraba en una entrevista que "empecinarse en mantener el referéndum es una gran equivocación". Aseguraba que dicho error debía "pagarlo el gobierno de su bolsillo" y condicionaba "pedir que se vote" a la formulación de una pregunta "que no cierre el futuro" y no suponga la aprobación de la política exterior gubernamental.
h. Tras una serie de averiguaciones policiales se supo la fecha y el lugar de llegada de un yate gallego que iba a desembarcar en la isla un importante cargamento de droga.

i. Y Celia pudo comprobarlo durante la ocupación del pueblo, cuando un muchacho gallego anunció en la plaza de la parroquia que deseaba abandonar la guerrilla, que no aguantaba más.

j. Un catalán o un gallego podrían pertenecer al equipo de España.

The phoneme /ɟ/

11. Read the following words and decide if the ll is pronounced [ɟ] or [ʝ].

anillo	maullar	fallar	taller	el llanto
billar	enllavar	botella	silla	la llorona
detalle	conllevar	lluvia	sin llaves	las llamas

12. Read the following words and decide if the y is pronounced [ɟ] or [ʝ].

ayer	mayas	inyectar	payaso	desayuno
cuyo	enyugar	el yogur	concluyó	yerba
yo	cónyuge	con yoga	la yema	haya

Final exercise

13. Read the following sentences taken from different newspapers and pay attention to the pronunciation of b/v, d, g, and ll/y in different phonetic contexts.

a. Además, una ofensiva creíble para la pacificación y la modernización de estos países debe ir de la mano de un diálogo.

b. Las democracias tienen la obligación de demostrar mediante sus actos, que realmente son democracias.

c. Fue trasladado a un hospital, pero no tiene ninguna herida de gravedad.

d. Dada la necesidad de consultas y de discusiones adicionales con los acreedores, es difícil establecer un preciso cronograma para lanzar y completar la oferta.

e. Debemos salir de esta reunión con decisiones.

f. *La mala educación* es la decimoquinta película de Pedro Almodóvar.

g. Saint-Exupéry desapareció después de partir de la isla de Córcega a bordo de su avión para una misión de reconocimiento cuyo objetivo era hallar información sobre los movimientos de las tropas alemanas, y destinada a preparar el desembarco aliado en Provenza.

h. Con la suficiente velocidad, un vehículo espacial puede liberarse de la gravedad terrestre y entrar en una órbita alrededor del Sol, como la de un planeta.

i. El cava y el champán son dos vinos espumosos de gran personalidad. Se distinguen por su linaje y estilo, el suelo donde arraigan las vides, las uvas que los producen y el método de elaboración. Todo ello les aporta..., el tamaño de la burbuja y su expresión aromática.

j. Esta es la excavación más grande llevada a cabo desde 1986. Ya se han revelado partes considerables de la ciudad romana, que estuvo poblada también en el período bizantino y el árabe antiguo. Paralelamente, los arqueólogos volvieron a excavar en la antigua colina donde se levantaba la ciudad en la Edad de Bronce.

9

The sibilant fricative /s/

In this chapter, we describe the phoneme /s/. (The **PHONEME** concept has been explained in Chapter 1.). The corresponding allophones are fricatives.

Today, most Spanish speakers (everybody in the Americas, the Canary Islands, and most Andalusians) do not distinguish the pronunciation of **s**, **z** and **c** (before **e** + **i**). This phenomenon is called **SESEO** and reminds us of the independence of pronunciation from orthography.

The letter **z** at the beginning of words, between vowels and at the end of words, is never pronounced as a voiced [z], as can be heard sometimes from English natives who say **[z]ócalo**, **Vene[z]uela**, **cerve[z]a**, **die[z]**, etc.

In most cases, **s**, **z** and **c** (before **e** + **i**) represent voiceless alveolar fricatives [s]. The only exceptions are **s**, **z** before voiced consonants, which, due to ASSIMILATION, are pronounced as voiced alveolar fricatives, [z].

The phoneme /s/

[z] VOICED ALVEOLAR FRICATIVE

ONLY before VOICED consonants: **desde** [ˈdez.ðe], **Lisboa** [liz.ˈβo.a], **rasgo** [ˈraz.ɣo], **asno** [ˈaz.no], **chisme** [ˈchiz.me], **portazgo** [poɾ.ˈtaz.ɣo], **las damas** [laz.ˈða.mas]

[s] VOICELESS ALVEOLAR FRICATIVE

All other contexts: **cinco** [ˈsiŋ.ko], **seis** [ˈsejs], **español** [es.pa.ˈɲol], **estructura** [es.truk.ˈtu.ra], **buscar** [bus.ˈkar], **descripción** [des.krip.ˈsjon], **voz** [ˈbos], **feroz** [fe.ˈroz], **las flores** [las.ˈflo.res]

You can use the sound [s] instead of [z] in words like **asno** and **mismo**, as many Spanish speakers do it, but it is almost impossible in words like **desde**.

As we have mentioned in Chapter 6, because it takes a lot of articulatory effort and strong air flow to produce friction, this sound tends to be altered or even dropped in many contexts and situations. WEAKENING and **ASPIRATION** (substitution by the glottal fricative sound [h]) of /s/ at the end of words is the norm among educated speakers in many countries and regions, for example in the Canary Islands, the Caribbean, the north, Golf and Pacific coasts of Mexico, El Salvador, Honduras, Nicaragua, Panama, the lowlands of Bolivia, Chile, Argentina, Paraguay, and Uruguay. Weakening and complete loss at the end of non-word-final syllables, is more typical in certain regions and social groups. You will find more information about this in Chapter 17.

The [z] sound is usually aspirated or dropped in some words before an [r] sound, the only frequent word being the name **Israel** [ir.a.'el]. This is not a regional pronunciation; it happens because it is difficult to pronounce it otherwise. The complete loss of the [s] sound can produce homophones, words that sound alike but have different meanings, but there are only a couple of words where this happens, for example **desramar** (*to remove the limbs from a tree*) [de.ra.'mar] vs. **derramar** (*to spill*) [de.ra.'mar]. If the context does not disambiguate the meaning, one still has the option of pronouncing the word slowly: des-ra-mar. The aspiration or loss of [s] can also happen in phonological phrases where one word ends in **s** and the other starts with **r**, for example **las ramas** → [la.'ra.mas].

The phoneme /s/ is written **s** before any vowel and **z** + any vowel. Both letters can also be found at the end of words: **sábado, secular, siniestro, soler, supremo, carros; Zamora, Zócalo, cazuela; crisis, libros, avestruz, actriz**. It can also be written **c** before **e/i**: **hace, cimiento**.

At the beginning of words from Greek, for example **xenofobia, xerocopia, xilófono**, etc., the **x** is pronounced [s]. In informal speech, before consonants, there are also other words where the **x** can sound [s], for example **extra** [es.tra]. This pronunciation is optional and depends on many factors.

The [z] sound is also written either **s** or **z: desde, esdrújula, asbesto, resbalar, riesgo, rasgo, uzbeco, hallazgo, juzgar**, etc.

In northern and central Spain there is another sibilant called **APICAL s**, that is sometimes transcribed with the phonetic symbol [s̱]. As the name suggests, it is articulated with the tip of the tongue (Span. ÁPICE DE LA LENGUA) and not with the larger front of the tongue as in other parts of Spain and all of Latin America. To produce the apical **s**, which is very common in Castilian Spanish, the tongue is concave, curved with the tip of the tongue up, as if you are trying to touch your nose with the tip of your tongue. However, you do not touch the nose, but the back of the alveolar ridge.

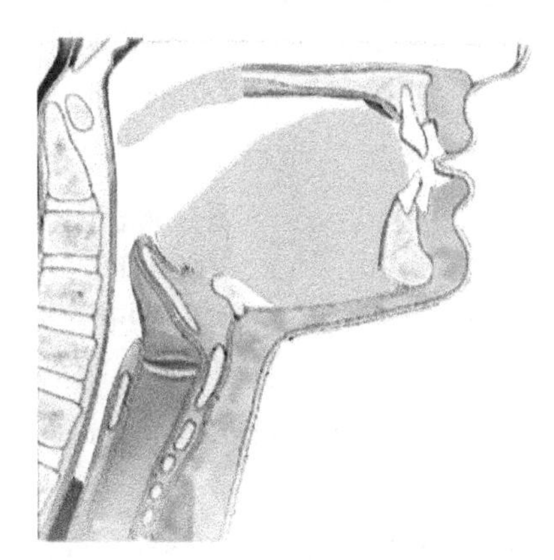

The predorsal [s] *(America and parts of Spain)*

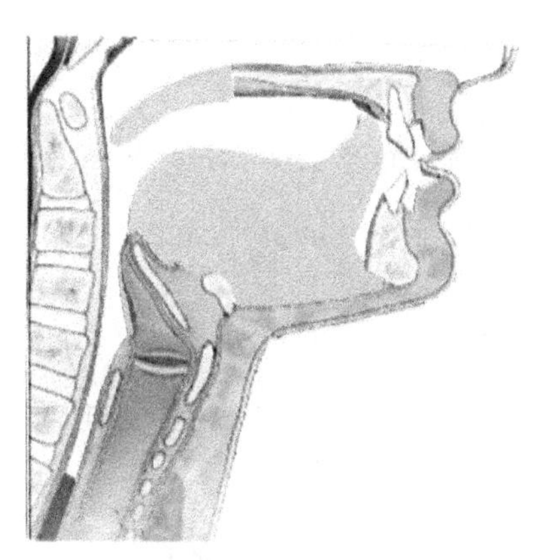

The apical [s̱] *(Central and Northern Spain)*

The phoneme /θ/

In Central and Northern Spain, many speakers pronounce the letters **z** and **c** (before **e**, **i**) like the English **th** in therapy, with the voiceless interdental fricative [θ] sound. Here, words with different meanings such as **casa** ['ka.sa] (house) and **caza** ['ka.θa] (hunt), paso ['pa.so] (step, pace) and **pazo** ['pa.θo] (*type of farmhouse in Galicia*) are pronounced differently. Most speakers in the south of Spain and the Canary Islands do not use the [θ] sound. There are, however, pockets where people distinguish [s] and [θ], such as in Central and Northern Spain. The [θ] sound is a relatively recent development in Spanish, from around the 16th and 17th centuries.

[θ] also undergoes assimilation before a voiced consonant, so just like /s/ becomes [z] in those contexts, /θ/ becomes [ð]. So the words **uzbeco**, **hallazgo** and **juzgar** are pronounced [uð.'βe.ko], [a.'ʝað.ɣo] and [xuð.'ɣaɾ].

There are also people that pronounce all the graphemes "s", "c" +"e, i" and "z" + "a, o, u" with [θ]. Some examples are **seco** ['θe.ko], **casa** ['ka.θa], **caza** ['ka.θa], **centro** ['θen̪.tro], **zona** ['θo.na]. This is called **CECEO** [θe.'θe.o].

This means that in some parts of Spain there are at least (5) sibilants:

[s]	voiceless predorsal alveolar fricative
[s̺]	voiceless apical alveolar fricative
[θ]	voiceless interdental fricative
[z]	voiced predorsal alveolar fricative
[ð]	voiced interdental fricative

For speakers that distinguish /s/ and /θ/ these sounds are part of two separate families, i.e. are two distinct phonemes, because they distinguish words with different meanings, for example **abrasar** (to burn) vs. **abrazar** (*to hug*), **asar** (to roast) vs. **azar** (luck); **seda** (silk) vs. **ceda** (Subj. of to cede); **segar** (to reap) vs. **cegar** (to blind); **Sena** (the river 'Seine') vs. **cena** (dinner); **sesión** (session) vs. **cesión** (cession); **sien** (*temple*) vs. **cien** (hundred); **siento** (I feel) vs. **ciento** (one hundred); **sierra** (mountain range or saw) vs. **cierra** (he/ she closes); **sima** (chasm) vs. **cima** (summit); **consejo** (advice) vs. **concejo** (council); **sebo** (tallow) vs. **cebo** (bait); **seta** (mushroom) vs. **zeta** (the letter *zee*); **ves** (you see) vs. **vez** (time); **vos** (you) vs. **voz** (voice); etc.

The phonemes /s/ and /z/ in English

In English there are two phonemes, /s/ and /z/, something that you can see easily in the pairs face and phase, bus and buzz.

/s/

[s] VOICELESS ALVEOLAR FRICATIVE

at the beginning of words: sink [ˈsɪŋk]

between vowels: racer, [ˈɹeɪ.sɚ] rice [ˈɹaɪs], precedent [ˈpɹɛ.sə.dɛnt]

at the end of words: bus [ˈbʌs]

/z/

[z] VOICED ALVEOLAR FRICATIVE

at the beginning of words: zink [ˈzɪŋk]

between vowels: razor [ɹeɪ.zɚ], rise [ˈɹaɪz], president [ˈpɹɛ.zə.dɛnt]

at the end of words: buzz [ˈbʌz]

Let's practice

You should not have any problems with the phoneme /s/ in Spanish if you follow the rules below:

1. Always pronounce the letters **s**, **c** (before **e**, **i**) and **z**, independently from the context, as **[s]**, just like in the English words six, best, his, etc.

2. Because of the process of assimilation, an **s** becomes voiced automatically before voiced consonants, for example **b**, **d**, **g** and nasals. You often do not need to make a conscious effort to do this.

3. If **z** is followed by a vowel, it should not be pronounced as a voiced [z] such as in the English words `zoom`, `zoo`, `blaze` or `buzz`. Before voiced consonants, for example in **hazlo**, follow rule 2.

4. In more formal situations, for example in presentations and speeches, try to pronounce every **s**. In informal speech or when you talk very fast, it is acceptable to aspirate final **s** when necessary and possible.

5. Be careful with words like **visual**, **usual**, **casual**, **sensual,** and **controversial**, that are spelled the same way in both Spanish and English, but pronounced differently, with the sounds [ʒ] and [ʃ] in English.

Exercises

1. The letter c before e and i is pronounced [s] in most dialects of Spanish. Read the following words.

acepción	decepción	recepción
adolescencia	docencia	Cicerón
concepto	excepción	ejercicio
complacencia	inocencia	piececitas
concepción	licencia	superficie
creencia	percepción	obcecación

2. Pronounce the following pairs of English and Spanish words. Remember that in Spanish s and z (Latin America) in these environments are always voiceless.

INGLÉS	ESPAÑOL	INGLÉS	ESPAÑOL
basilica	basílica	resolve	resolver
Caesar	César	result	resultado
phase	fase	rose	rosa
physically	físicamente	visit	visita
music	música	zenith	cenit
nasal	nasal	zinc	cinc
reserve	reserva	Zodiac	Zodíaco
resident	residente	zebra	cebra
residue	residuo	zone	zona
resignation	resignación	Byzantine	bizantino
resist	resistir	base	base

2. Are the letters s and z in the following examples voiced or voiceless?

cacicazgo	juzgar	Esto nos dice mucho
comadrazgo	liderazgo	son las diez del día
compadrazgo	lloviznar	son las doce del día
desdecir	noviazgo	las dotes de mando
desdén	sin rasgo	los dos duros de Juan
desdicho	les debo dinero	las dudas de María
durazno	los dejo aquí	muchos daños graves
esdrújula	las damas danesas	
hallazgo	los días del año	

4. The letter x in the following examples can be pronounced [s] or [ks].

extra	excéntrico	inexperiencia
mixto	excepcional	exportar
textiles	excitación	sexto lugar
excarcelar	exclamar	texto
excavar	excluir	extinción
exceder	extrovertido	externo
excelencia	inexcusable	

5. The letters s or ss followed by u or i in English are sometimes pronounced [ʃ] or [ʒ] and not [s]. Read the following pairs of words.

INGLÉS	ESPAÑOL	INGLÉS	ESPAÑOL
visual	visual	magnesia	magnesia
usual	usual	pleasure	placer
casual	casual	lesion	lesión
treasure	tesoro	fissure	fisura
Asia	Asia	mission	misión
Indonesia	Indonesia	vision	visión

Final exercise

6. Read the following sentences.

a. Creo que la experiencia de la infancia es muy superior a la de la adolescencia.

b. Las veintitrés piececitas de este registro, breves, sencillas, inspiradas y honestamente andalucistas, revelan a un músico que supo encontrar su sitio.

c. La nueva línea se ha diseñado para una velocidad máxima de trescientos kilómetros por hora, con excepción de varias restricciones a doscientos cuarenta kilómetros por hora en algunos tramos de curvas existentes en Módena.

d. La auténtica oposición ha sido físicamente destruida en los famosos procesos que han esmaltado el régimen de Hassan II, en las ejecuciones y las persecuciones como consecuencia de los complots y, en caso necesario, con truculencias como el asesinato de Ben Barka en París.

e. El canciller hondureño Delmer Panting dijo a periodistas de su país que las fuerzas de seguridad de Honduras, desplegadas en la zona fronteriza con El Salvador, tienen orden de capturar a los salvadoreños que talen el bosque ilegalmente.

10

Fricatives /f/, /x/, and affricate /tʃ/

The phoneme /f/

[f] VOICELESS LABIODENTAL FRICATIVE

fruta [ˈfru.ta], **feo** [ˈfe.o], **flor** [ˈfloɾ], **confesar** [koɱ.fe.ˈsaɾ], **difícil** [di.ˈfi.sil], etc.

The phoneme /f/ has only one allophone: [f]. It is always written with the grapheme **f**. Just like in English, it is a voiceless labiodental fricative sound. In English, it occurs in positions: `five`, `office`, `after`, `golf`, etc. In Spanish, on the other hand, it is used almost exclusively at the beginning of words and syllables. There is no native Spanish word that ends with [f]. The around twenty (20) words that are included in the Dictionary of the Royal Spanish Language Academy and in the Diccionario de uso del español by María Moliner, are taken from other languages or are loan words, for example **golf**, **surf**, **turf**, **rosbif**, etc.

In some local dialects and sociolects, for example on the Atlantic Coast of Colombia, **f** can be weakened and sound similar to [β], a voiceless approximant that is often transcribed with the symbol [ɸ].

There are no practice exercises for this sound because it is no different from the English /f/.

The phoneme /tʃ/

[tʃ] VOICELESS PREPALATAL AFFRICATE

chico [ˈtʃi.ko], **coche** [ˈko.tʃe], **chucho** [ˈtʃu.tʃo], **chulo** [ˈtʃu.lo], etc.

The phoneme /tʃ/ is the only affricate phoneme in Spanish. It has only one allophone, the voiceless prepalatal affricate sound [tʃ] that combines a complete closure with friction, the two sounds [t] and [ʃ]. Therefore, it is not a coincidence that it is distinctive from stop phonemes, such as /t/, and fricative phonemes like /s/, for example in the series **chaco** - **taco** - **saco** or **hacha** - **ata** - **asa**.

It is always written with the grapheme **ch** and sounds very much like the sound [tʃ] in the English words `chair, which, achieve, factual, twitch, manufacture`, where it can be written in different ways. A minor difference between the two languages is due to the effect of assimilation in Spanish, which causes the place of articulation of the [t] to move closer to that of [ʃ]. In English, the place of articulation of the [t] is more alveolar.

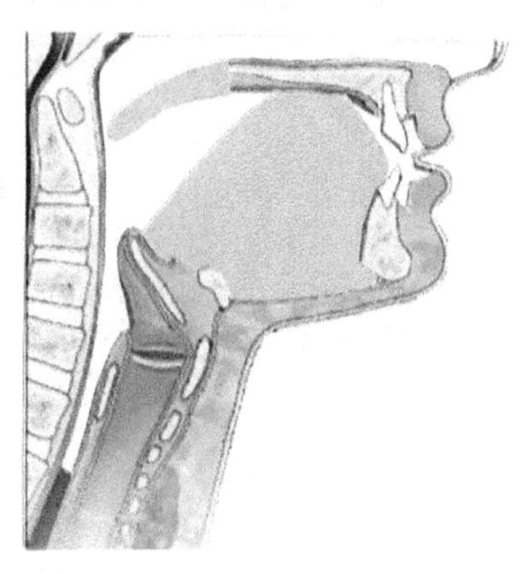

The voicelss prepalatal affricate sound [tʃ]

The sound [tʃ] is only used at the beginning of words and syllables. There are no native Spanish words that end in **ch** either. The few examples are new loan words from other languages. The most popular ones are **brunch** and **sandwich**.

In some Spanish speaking areas in the world, for example in parts of Andalusia and also in Latin America, some speakers reduce the affricate sound [tʃ] to the simple fricative sound [ʃ], and don't say ['tʃi.ko] but ['ʃi.ko].

There are no practice exercises for this sound either, again because of its similarity to the English affricate /tʃ/.

The phoneme /x/

[x] VOICELESS VELAR FRICATIVE

written **j** before any vowel: **jamón** [xa.ˈmon], **jefe** [ˈje.ˈfe], **bajito** [ba.ˈxi.to], **bajo** [ˈba.xo], **conjugar** [koŋ.xu.ˈgaɾ]

written g before **e** and **i: Gilberto** [xil.ˈβeɾ.to], **coger** [ko.ˈxeɾ]

written **x** in a few words: **México** [ˈme.xi.ko], **Oaxaca** [wa.ˈxa.ka]

The phoneme /x/ has only the allophone [x], a voiceless velar fricative sound that doesn't exist in English. This allophone is written with the letters **j**, g, and **x.** (See Chapter 2 about Spelling.)

There are very few words in Spanish that end with **–j**. The only popular one is **reloj**. In this final position, however, the **j** is almost never pronounced. In the plural form **relojes**, on the other hand, you can hear it.

In Central and Northern Spain, many people pronounce this allophone as a postvelar or uvular sound with a lot of friction. In a more detailed transcription, this sound is represented with the symbol [χ].

In the south of Spain, the Canary Islands and Latin America, this allophone is velar and is produced with less friction, but with more tension of the tongue. Many times, when the pronunciation is even more relaxed and the sound is produced further back in the mouth, in glottal position, it sounds like an aspirated [h], similar to the [h] in head or as [xʰ], an [x] with velar friction followed by an aspiration. The different pronunciations of the [x] sound are regional and are independent from the phonetic environment.

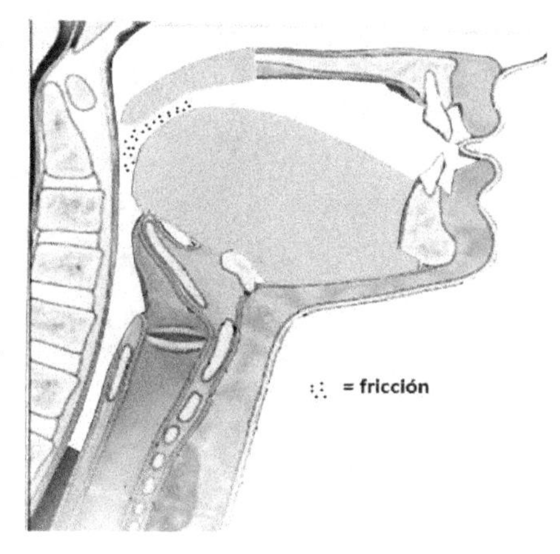

The sound [χ] (parts of Spain)

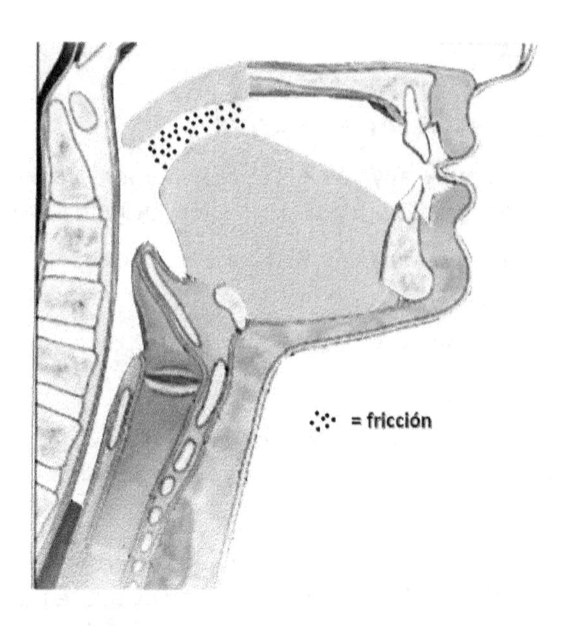

The [x] sound (Canary Islands and Latin America)

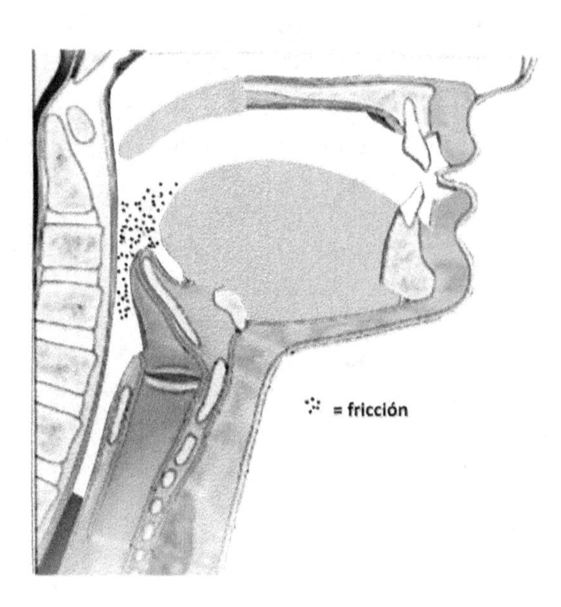

The [h] sound (Latin America, especially the Caribbean)

Exercises

1. **A g before e and i are pronounced [x]. Read the following examples.**

ángel	escoger	página	región
agitar	exigir	surgir	rígido
acoger	fingir	virgen	ungido
coger	frágil	gemelo	vigilar
colegio	gel	género	angina
elegir	gil	genial	lógico
elogio	imagen	gente	
emergencia	magia	gira	
energía	margen	gitano	
erigir	origen	Ángela	

2. **2. [g] or [x]?**

ligero	Georgia	aguajero	juego
geólogo	ginecóloga	agujero	jugador
demagogia	griego	ajeno	jugoso
gigante	negligencia	anglosajón	juzgado
geológico	genético	cangrejo	lagartijo
pedagogía	regiones	granja	lenguaje
gigantesco	agasajar	granjero	mujeriego
agregar	agigantar	jaguar	reciclaje
geógrafa	agregar	jerga	pasaje

Final exercise

3. **Read the following sentences taken from various newspapers. Pay attention to the pronunciation of the letters g and j.**

a. Aseguró que no hacía demagogia al señalar que es paradójico que estas propuestas lingüísticas las proponga un partido que tiene en su seno a los representantes de las oligarquías que en su día expulsaron de su tierra a una gente que tuvo que venir a Cataluña a ganarse el pan.

b. Ahora lo lamentamos porque el supuesto tráfico o traslado ilegal de menores a Venezuela, refleja nuestra negligencia a todo nivel: policial, jurídica, socioeconómica.

c. Primera novela del poeta Juan Bonilla, *Nadie conoce a nadie* (Ediciones B) es una extensa y ambiciosa obra que narra la engañosa y difícil relación de dos personajes obsesionados por la literatura. Al fondo, una compleja maquinaria terrorista convertida en un gigantesco juego de rol que alguien maneja a su antojo.

d. Un mes antes de que su padre abandonara el cargo, relajada y sonriente, con varios cambios de vestuario, Zulemita le dio un extenso reportaje a la revista *Caras*, su preferida. A Zulemita le fascinaba el estilo del semanario de *Perfil*. Fotos grandes y un lenguaje ligero. Amaba verse reflejada en sus páginas.

11

Rhotics /ɾ/ and /r/

One of the biggest differences between English and Spanish is the pronunciation of **r** or **rr**. English speakers who learn Spanish, often have problems producing the respective sounds, because they are so different from English. The [ɹ] sound in American English is produced either by the retroflexion of the tip of the tongue towards the area between the alveolar ridge and the hard palate (= **RETROFLEX R**) or by lifting both sides of the back of the tongue towards the upper molars. The latter option is called **BUNCHED R** because the tongue is bunched and retracts towards the throat.

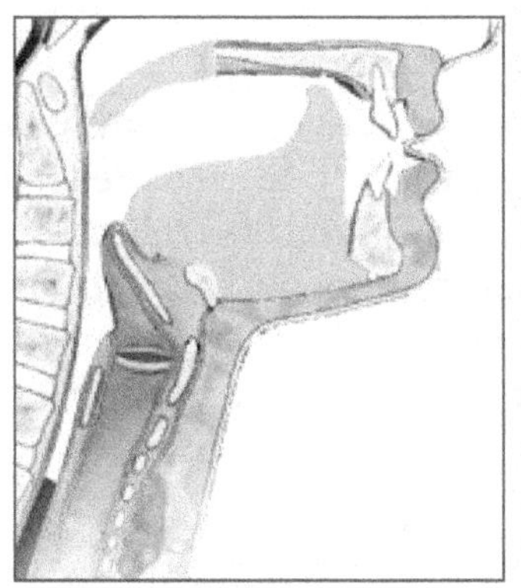

Retroflex r

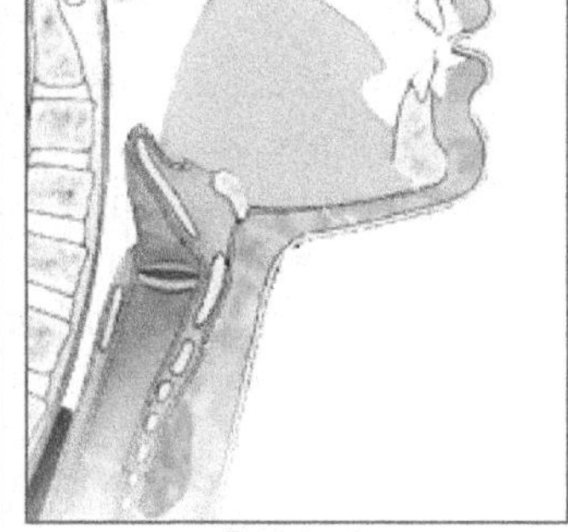

Bunched r

Because the American [ɹ] has no phonetic equivalent in any of the European languages, it represents a substantial obstacle for anyone trying to learn American English.

Both **r**, /ɾ/ and /r/ in Spanish are alveolar sounds formed with the front of the tongue and the alveolar ridge (Span. **ALVÉOLOS**) Those familiar with Scottish English will find these sounds to be similar to the Scottish **r**. There are two rhotics phonemes in Spanish: one with a single tap (or flap): /ɾ/, and one with multiple taps or trills of the tongue: /r/

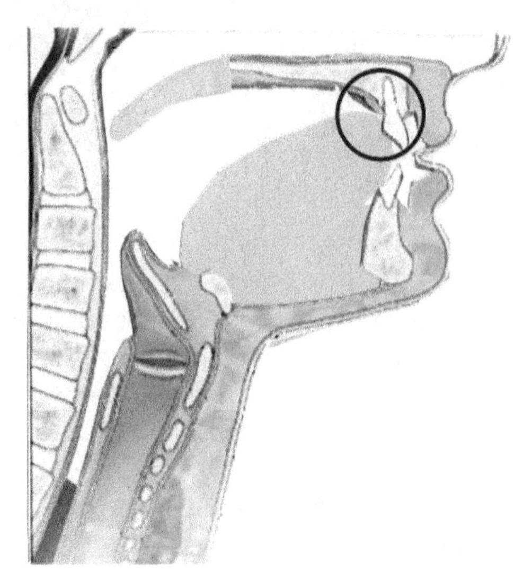

Alveolar r

The letter **r** at the beginning of words or **rr** within words is ALWAYS pronounced [r] (with multiple taps or trills). It would be redundant to write words like **rima**, **Roma** or **rana** with a double **rr**, because speakers know that, in this position, it is always pronounced with a trill. The pronunciation does not change even when the **r** is preceded by another word: **la rana** = [la.'ra.na], **las ranas** = [las.'ra.nas], **mil ranas** = [mil.'ra.nas], **edad real** = [e.'ðað.re.'al].

Words written with **rr** between vowels are pronounced with a trill, and their meaning is distinguished from words written with just one intervocalic **r**, which is pronounced with a simple tap ([ɾ]). The [r] and [ɾ] sounds here contrast to give words different meanings, for example: **caro** vs. **carro**, **pero** vs. **perro**. This means that, theoretically, and with the important exception of **r** at the beginning of words, it is only necessary to produce a trill (multiple vibrations of the tongue) when you see double **rr**. If you were to pronounce all the single letters **r** with just one tap or vibration of the tongue, similar to the pronunciation of the **d** or the **t** in English, words like `better` and `edit`, Spanish speakers would understand you perfectly. Furthermore, there is a lot of variation in the production of the sounds [r] and [ɾ] in the Spanish speaking world, as you will see in Chapter 17.

Whether the letter **r** is produced with a single flap or a trill depends basically on the position of the sound within the word. Normally, there is a trill, obligatory or optional, AT THE BEGINNING OF WORDS AND SYLLABLES:

1. Obligatory: **roto**, **rama**, etc.
2. Optional: after alveolar consonants **l**, **n**, **s**: **al-re-de-dor**, **hon-ra**, **Is-ra-el**

Typically, there is only a single flap when an **r** doesn´t start a new syllable. As you saw in Chapter 3, the consonant combinations or clusters **br, dr, gr, pr, tr, cr** and **fr** in Spanish are never divided, and we said that when a particular consonant cluster can start a word, it can also start a new syllable: a-**br**a-zo, a-**dr**e-na-li-na, in-gre-sar, a-**pr**en- der, a-**tr**as, a-**cr**ó-ba-ta, a-**fr**i-ca-no, etc. Therefore, in the combinations **br, dr, gr, pr, tr, cr** and **fr**, **r** is pronunced [ɾ]. This also goes for word and syllable end position: á**r**-bol, a-ba**r**-ca, a**r**-de, ma**r**-fil, ma**r**-gen, a-ma**r**-go, bu**r**-lar, a**r**-ma, ca**r**-ne, ca**r**-pa, pa**r**-que, a**r**-se-nal, sue**r**-te, ce**r**-ve-za, Da**r**-win, etc. In this position, the trill (multiple vibrations) has an emphatic meaning: "**No vamos a perder, ¡vamos a ganarrrrr!**".

The only position where the two phonemes /r/ and /ɾ/ can be interchangeable and modify the meaning is between vowels (intervocalic position): **caro** vs. **carro**; **ahora** vs. **ahorra**. The difference is also reflected in writing with the graphemes **r** and **rr**. None of the other positions entails phonological contrast.

The phoneme /r/

[r] VOICED ALVEOLAR TRILL

between vowels: **carro** (always written **rr**)

word-initial position: **rosa, las rosas, edad real**

syllable-initial position, after alveolar consonants **l**, **n**, **s**: **hon-ra**, **Is-ra-el**

emphatic pronunciation: at the end of words)typically only at the en of utterances: **mi amorrr**

The phoneme /ɾ/

[ɾ] VOICED ALVEOLAR TRILL

between vowels: **caro** (always written **r**)

in consonant clusters **br, dr, r, pr, tr, cr** and **fr:** a-**bra**-zo, a-**dre**-na-li-na, in-gre-sar, a-**pren**-der, a-**tras**, a-**cró**-ba-ta, a-**fri**-ca-no, etc.

in syllable-final position: á**r**-bol, a-ba**r**-ca, a**r**-de, ma**r**-fil, ma**r**-gen, a-ma**r**-go, bu**r**-lar, a**r**-ma, ca**r**-ne, ca**r**-pa, pa**r**-que, a**r**-se-nal, sue**r**-te, ce**r**-ve-za, Da**r**-win, etc.

in word-final position: No vamos a gan**ar**.

Let's practice!

You have already seen that the Spanish [ɾ] sound also exists in English, where it is written **t**, **tt**, **d** and **dd** between stressed and unstressed vowels, for example in **city**, **later**, **better**, **lady**, **edit**, **ladder**, etc. Now you just need to get accustomed to the new spelling as **r**. A good exercise could be pronouncing the words **tres** and **tren** without moving the tongue. Then, you can do the same exercises with the words **tereno**, **Teresa**, **terapia**.

Once you have learned to pronounce the [ɾ] sound in words like **cara**, **abre**, **cargo**, you can switch to practicing the [r] sound, with multiple vibrations of the tip of the tongue (= trill) in words like **carro**, **rosa**, **alrededor**, etc. by maintaining the place of articulation of the [ɾ] sound.

The production of the [r] sound with several vibrations of the tongue can be a big problem for English speakers. There are several methods for producing the alveolar trill. Here is one: Try to articulate a **p** without opening the mouth. Then, when you open the mouth, quickly touch the incisors with the tip of your tongue as if you wanted to produce an **l**. Relax your tongue and keep it flat; being careful not to curve it back. Repeat this exercise until you get your tongue to vibrate. Most importantly, the tip of your tongue must be relaxed. The vibration of the tongue is produced in the same way as in the following experiment: Get a sheet of paper of around 3 X 7 inches, hold the corners of the short side with the index finger and the thumb of both hands, hold the short side just below your lower lip and blow until the sheet starts to vibrate.

Exercises

1. **Read the following series of words. If you replace the r mentally with an English d, you should be able to pronounce the Spanish [ɾ] correctly.**

práctica	practicable	practicante
pradeña	pradera	pradejón
precario	precariamente	precariedad
preceder	precedente	precedencia
precioso	preciosa	preciosamente
pregunta	preguntar	preguntador
premio	premiar	premiación
prenda	prender	prendido
prensa	prensar	prensado
prueba	probar	aprobado

2. **Pronounce the following words. The Spanish [ɾ] sounds exactly like the English t, tt or dd in `later`, `better`, *`get up`*, *`ladder`*, `header`. If there is a vowel before or after the r, try to stretch it out a little longer than in English and keep the vowel articulation full and clear.**

caro	baro	cara	pirineo
lera	hierba	era	erizo
lempira	llorar	barba	barco
perilla	extra	pero	Ebro
obra	piedra	África	comprar
otro	agrio	Carmen	largo
ofrenda	aprieto	Ucrania	abrir

3. **Pronounce the initial r with a trill of the tongue. If you have problems pronouncing the combination [sr], you can aspirate or omit the s of the plural articles.**

la rabia	las rabias	la rama	las ramas
el rabo	los rabos	la rana	las ranas
la ración	las raciones	el rancho	los ranchos
el radar	los radares	el rango	los rangos
la raíz	las raíces	la rebaja	las rebajas
el rallo	los rallos	la red	las redes

el riesgo	los riesgos	la ropa	las ropas
el rigor	los rigores	la rosa	las rosas
la rima	las rimas	la rosca	las roscas
el río	los ríos	el rubí	los rubíes
la risa	las risas	la rueda	las ruedas
el rival	los rivales	el ruido	los ruidos
el roble	los robles	la ruina	las ruinas
el robo	los robos	la rumba	las rumbas
la roca	las rocas	el rumbo	los rumbos
el rocío	los rocíos	el rumor	los rumores
el rodeo	los rodeos	la runa	las runas
el ron	los rones	la ruta	las rutas

4. Read across. The first word on each line has an r with just a simple flap and the others have multiple vibrations or trills.

abrir	aburrir	aburre	burro
escaparate	parte	aparte	arte
probamos	borla	borrar	borroso
cráter	carril	Carlos	Carlota
cruel	corral	corta	corla
groso	gorro	ahorro	aorta
aparato	parto	esparto	harto
parado	parto	comparto	ortopedia
poroto	porto	aporto	la porra
perenal	perla	perra	emperrada

5. Pronounce the [ɾ] y [r] in the following pairs of words.

ahora	ahorra	mira	mirra
buró	burro	moro	morro
caro	corro	para	parra
cero	cerro	paro	parro
coro	corro	pera	perra
ere	erre	poro	porro
foro	forro	cura	curra
hiero	hierro	toro	torre
hora	horra	turón	turrón

6. **Read the following tongue twisters.**

- Borracho un ratón robó un ramo de rosas rojas.
- El rabo se le enredó y rodó de rosa en rosa.
- Jorge el cerrajero vende cerrajes en la cerrajería.
- Rosa Rizo reza en ruso, en ruso reza Rosa Rizo.
- Un burro comía berros y el perro se los robó, el burro lanzó un rebuzno, y el perro al barro cayó.
- Parra tenía una perra. Guerra tenía una parra. La perra de Parra subió a la parra de Guerra.
- Guerra pegó con la porra a la perra de Parra.
- Y Parra le dijo a Guerra: ¿Por qué ha pegado Guerra con la porra a la perra de Parra? Y Guerra le contestó: Si la perra de Parra no hubiera subido a la parra de Guerra,
- Guerra no habría pegado con la porra a la perra de Parra.

- Erre con erre, cigarro;

  erre con erre, barril;

  rápido ruedan los carros

  por los rieles del ferrocarril.

- El perro de San Roque no tiene rabo porque Ramón Ramírez se lo ha cortado.
- El perro de Ramón Ramírez no tiene rabo porque se lo han robado.
- ¿Quién le ha robado el rabo al perro de San Roque?
- Ramón Ramírez ha robado el rabo del perro de San Roque.
- El terrateniente Ramón Pueyrredón Aguirre arreaba rumiantes en su remoto rancho.

- Se aburría Ramón encerrado en su recurrente rutina.
- Resuelto a romperla, arrancó rumbo a tierras rimbombantes.

- 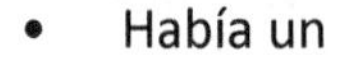 Había un 

  debajo de un 

  vino otro 

  y le mordió el 

- Corre por la calle arriba,
  corre, corre por la calle abajo.

- Por la calle de Carretas
  pasaba un perrito;
  pasó una carreta y
  le pisó el rabito.
  ¡Pobre perrito,
  cómo lloraba
  por su rabito!

- Rosa Rosales cortó una rosa. ¡Que roja la rosa de Rosa Rosales!
- El burrito barrigón ayer se dio un resbalón.
- Por andar detrás de un carro, se cayó dentro del barro.
- ¡Qué burrito picarón, el burrito barrigón!

Final exercise

7. Read the following sentences.

a. El amplificador pertenecía a otro radiorreceptor mucho más grande que el que posee.

b. Ese viaje fue su reencuentro con el Perú profundo y el primero de una serie interminable que lo llevó a recorrer el país de cabo a rabo.

c. Los autores explican que la inexistencia de fuentes escritas que hagan referencia específica a la vida de los ferroviarios ha hecho necesario recurrir a las fuentes orales, y más concretamente a entrevistas realizadas a los trabajadores que han desarrollado la totalidad de su vida profesional en la Red Nacional de Ferrocarriles Españoles.

d. Ante el poder económico del frente Domingo Laín y la rebeldía de varios frentes en cinco regiones de Colombia, el cura Pérez aceptó reestructurar el Ejército de Liberación Nacional y tratar de conjurar una división al interior de la organización.

e. En Cuba, se considera que el consumo de los refrigeradores puede representar entre 30 y 50 por ciento del consumo en el sector residencial.

f. En la práctica, lo que el Ministerio de Ciencia y Tecnología, en coordinación con el área de Universidades del Ministerio de Educación, está tratando de hacer es liquidar a muy corto plazo el programa Ramón y Cajal, y aprovechar la flexibilidad de la también controvertida Ley Orgánica de Universidades, de la que faltan por desarrollar múltiples decretos, entre ellos, el del profesorado, para tratar de reincorporar a los Ramón y Cajal como son los contratos para doctores investigadores, coinciden el rector y el representante de esta sección.

12

Nasals /m/, /n/, /ɲ/

These three (3) phonemes are grouped in the same chapter because they are all nasal phonemes. What distinguishes them from oral sounds is that most of the airflow exits via the nose, rather than the mouth. The phonemes /m/ and / p/, for example, have the same place of articulation: the lips, making them bilabial sounds, for which we close the lips completely. For **p** we open the lips before the next sound, for example the **a** of **papá**, and let the air out through the mouth. For the **m** in **mamá**, however, we leave the lips closed and force some of the air to exit through the nose before we open them for the next sound, in this case the **a**. The three nasal consonants are all voiced, but have different places of articulation.

The three (3) phonemes /m/, /n/, and /ɲ/ have a contrastive function in intervocalic position, at the beginning of syllables: **amo/ ano/ año**; **cama/ cana/ caña**; **camal/ canal/ cañal**; **doma/ dona/ doña**; **lama/ lana/ laña**; **lema/ lena/ leña**. However, there are relatively few examples of these " minimal triplets" . At the beginning of words there are even fewer examples because there are only 58 words in the dictionary that start with **ñ**. Two examples are **maco/ naco/ ñaco** and **mudo/ nudo/ ñudo**. As you can see, many of the words in the examples are not commonly used anymore. As a result of the evolution from Latin, there are only around 130 words in Spanish the end in **m**. All of them are loan words from other languages, for example **film** (from English) or scholarly words, for example **auditorium** (from Classical Latin). There are no words that end in **ñ**. The pronunciation of nasal allophones at the end of words does not have a contrastive function in Spanish.

The phoneme /m/

The phoneme /m/ is very simple, in that it is represented in writing by only one letter, **m** and it has only one allophone, [m]. The sound [m] is exactly the same in Spanish and English. Before the bilabial sounds [b] and [m], the sound [m] is also written **n**: **convivir** = [kom.bi.'βir]], but as we will see later in this chapter, this example represents an allophone of /n/.

[m] VOICED BILABIAL NASAL

m in any position: **mamá** [ma.ˈma], **amo** [ˈa.mo], **lámpara** [ˈlam.pa.ɾa], **film** [ˈfilm]

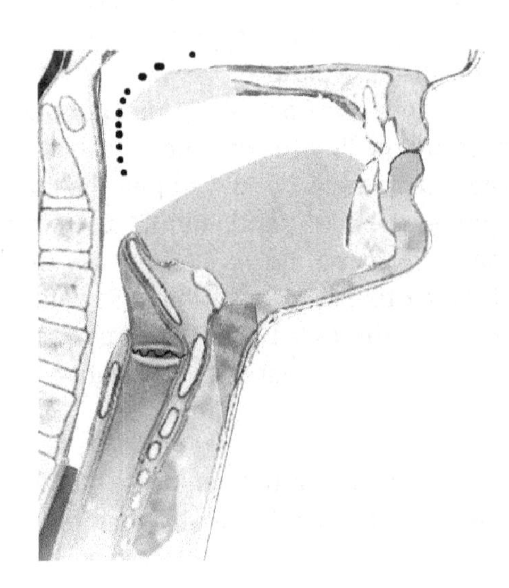

The phoneme /n/

The phoneme /n/ is more complicated because it has at least six (6) allophones –more than any other phoneme in Spanish– due to its adoption of the place of articulation of the consonant that follows: **tango** = ['taŋ.ɣo]. This phenomenon is called **ASSIMILATION**, which we saw in a different form —voicing assimilation— in Chapter 9, whereas here we have assimilation in place of articulation. Its purpose is to reduce the articulatory effort by shortening (or eliminating) the distance necessary to move from one place of articulation to another. There are different degrees of assimilation. If the places of articulation of two consonants are identical, there is complete assimilation, and the consonants are homorganic. In the case of **PARTIAL ASSIMILATION**, the places of articulation are close but not identical. Nasal assimilation in place of articulation only occurs at in coda position and has no contrastive phonological function.

In Spanish, assimilation is not limited to the word level: **informal** = [iɱfor'mal], but can also happen within phonological phrases, between words: **un fuego** = [uɱ.'fwe.ɣo]. Here it is not obligatory but variable.

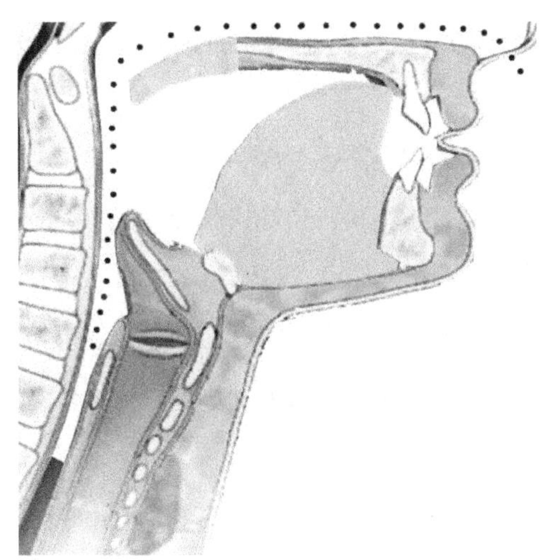

[n] VOICED ALVEOLAR NASAL

word-initially: ¡Nunca! ['nuŋ.ka]

before vowels: **Anita** [a.'ni.ta], **mano** ['ma.no], **vino** ['vi.no], **digno** ['diɣ.no], **balneario,** [bal.ne.'a.ɾjo], **carne** ['kaɾ.ne], **asno** ['az.no], **etnia** ['et.nja], **durazno** [du.'ɾaz.no], etc.

before alveolar consonants: **cansado** [kan.'sa.ðo], **enlace** [en.'la.se], **sonrisa** [son.'ri.sa]

Utterance-finally/ before a pause (or word-finally before alveolar consonants **¡No hablen!** [no.'a.βlen] **con redes** [kon.'re.ðes]

In many parts of Central America, the Caribbean, at the coasts of Venezuela, Colombia, and Mexico, and also in the south of Spain, it is common to hear the velar sound [ŋ] instead of [n] in this position, for example in the expression **¡Ven acá!** = [be.ŋa.'ka].

[m] **VOICED BILABIAL NASAL**

before **[p], [b], [m]**: **un pedazo** [um.pe.'ða.so], **enviar** [em.'bjaɾ], **convencer** [kom.ben.'ser], **inmenso** [im.'men.so]

[ɱ] **VOICED LABIODENTAL NASAL**

before **[f]**: énfasis ['eɱ.fa.sis], **enfermo** [eɱ.'feɾ.mo], **un fuego** [uɱ.'fwe.ɣo]

[n̪] **VOICED DENTAL NASAL**

before **[t], [d]**: **anda** ['an̪.da], **antes** ['an̪.tes], **han traído** ['an̪.tra.'i.ðo]

[ñ̪] **VOICED INTERDENTAL NASAL** (ONLY SPAIN)

before [θ]: **encinta** [eñ̪.'θin̪.ta], **encerrado** [eñ̪.θe.'ra.ðo], etc.

[ɲ] **VOICED PALATAL NASAL**

before **[ɟ]** and **[tʃ]**: **inyección** [iɲ.ɟek.'sjon], **cónyuge** ['koɲ.ɟu.xe], **con llave** [koɲ.'ɟa.βe], **ancho** ['aɲ.tʃo], **un chico** [uɲ.'tʃi.ko]

[ŋ] **VOICED VELAR NASAL**

before [**k, g, x**]: **ancla** ['aŋ.kla], **tengo** ['teŋ.go], **conjugar** [koŋ.xu.'ɣaɾ]

The [ŋ] sound is used within words but also when **n** is in word-final position and the next word starts with a velar sound, especially when people speak very fast: **un juego** [uŋ.'xwe.ɣo], **ven conmigo** ['beŋ.kom.'mi.ɣo].

Even though the duplication or gemination of consonants does not exist in most varieties of Spanish, there are around 90 learned and loan words that are written with **nn**, for example **connotar**, **ennoviarse**, **innato**, **innegable**. In relaxed speech, [nn] is often reduced to [n]: [in.ne.'ɣa.β|e] becomes [i.ne.›ɣa.β|e]. Sometimes this reduction is also reflected in writing: **innocuo/ inocuo**, **sunni/ suni**.

In many scholarly and loan words we can find the combination **ns + consonant**, for example **cir-cuns-tan-cia**, **trans-fe-ri-ble**, **ins-tin-to**, etc., with the group **ns** at the end of syllable. In many situations you can hear a weakening or even omission of the **n**: [sir.ku.'stan.sia], [tras. fe.'ri.βle], [is.'tin̪.to]. In some words with the prefix **trans-**, this reduction has been sanctioned in writing: **traspatio**, **trasfondo**, **trasmano**. When the prefix **trans-** is followed by an **s**, the two **s** become one: **tran-se-xual**, **tran-si-be-ria-no**.

The phoneme /ɲ/

[ɲ] **VOICED PALATAL NASAL**:

in all contexts: **niño** ['ni.ɲo], **año** ['a.ɲo], **ñañigo** [ɲa.'ɲi.ɣo], etc.

Let's practice

In English, we also have nasal assimilation before velar sounds: `anger, youngster, ping, sing, ink, increase` and before [f]: `emphasis, camphor, information`, but exclusively word-internally and NOT between words. In Spanish, on the other hand, the only context in which we don't assimilate is before a break or pause. Therefore, it is important in Spanish to link words that are part of a phonological phrase and not leave short pauses after every word.

Exercises

The phoneme /n/

1. **Read the following examples written with mp and mb line by line. Compilar and con Pilar must sound alike.**

combate	con bata
complacientes	con pacientes
compadecer la desgracia	con padecer la desgracia
compadre Ambrosio	con padre Ambrosio
comparar los coches	con parar los coches
comparte la casa	con parte de la casa
compasión	con pasión
compatriotas	con patriotas
complacer	con placer
compresa	con presa

2. **The sequence of letters nv is also pronounced [mb]. Con vino sounds exactly like combino and en vías like envías. Read the following list.**

convencer	convención	convencional	convenio
convenir	convento	convergencia	conversar
envase	enviar	envolver	invadir
inválido	invasión	inventar	invento
un vago	con validez	con valor	sin vino

3. **The n in énfasis is pronounced [ɱ]. Read the following list.**

confección	conflicto	conforme	confuso
enfermo	enfermera	enfadar	enfático
enfrentar	enfriar	infancia	infarto
infectar	infeliz	inferior	infinito
influencia	informe	infusión	ninfa

4. **Now pronounce the same consonant cluster between words.**

en forma	con factura	con facilidad	con falda
caer en falta	sin falta	en familia	un fantasma
un faro	con fiebre	con fecha	un film
un filósofo	sin fin	con flan	un filete
en Florencia	un fósforo	en Francia	con Félix

5. **The n before [tʃ] is pronounced [ɳ]. Read the following pairs of words.**

chico	un chico	chicano	un chicano
champú	un champú	chino	un chino
chaval	un chaval	chile	un chile
checo	un checo	chiste	un chiste
cheque	un cheque	chico	un chico

6. **Before [k], [g] and [x], word-internally, the n in Spanish is pronounced [ŋ], just like in the English word `finger`. Read the following pairs of words to hear and distinguish the difference between [n] and [ŋ].**

Ana	ancla	rana	rango
anular	angular	tenor	tengo
cono	Congo	vena	venga
canela	Ángela	viene	vengo
mono	hongo	vino	vínculo

7. **The same goes for n at the end of words and the sounds [k] and [g] at the beginning of the next word, when there is no pause between them.**

un gato	en Guinea	Carmen grita
un gran guía	un globo	con gusto
con ganas	cien godos	sin cambio
han ganado	un golpe	un café
tienen ganas	sin gozar	han caído
con gas	cien gramos	sin cambio
sin gas	sin grasa	con cobre
han gastado	con gripe	con gorro
un gasto	sin grifo	

8. Repeat these sets of words with dental [t] and [d] and then with dental [nt] and [nd].

ata	anda	padre	panda
beta	venda	pedir	pendiente
bota	bondad	pido	pinto
cada	anda	sede	sentir
cata	canta	sido	siento
codo	onda	tata	tanta
cuota	contra	Tito	tinto
dedo	dentro	zeta	centro
mata	manda	mido	miento

9. Read the following text about the military architect of Felipe II, Juan Bautista Antonelli, and pay attention to pronouncing all the allophones of /n/ correctly.

JUAN BAUTISTA ANTONELLI: ARQUITECTO DE LAS DEFENSAS DE FELIPE SEGUNDO EN VARIOS PAÍSES DE AMÉRICA

¿También te fascinan los corsarios o los piratas del Caribe? El siguiente texto es sobre un arquitecto militar que dedicó su vida para repeler a los piratas de los principales puertos españoles alrededor del Caribe en el siglo dieciséis y diecisiete.

A finales del siglo dieciséis incursiones de los corsarios franceses, ingleses y holandeses convencieron al rey Felipe Segundo de encargar a Juan Bautista Antonelli que realizara mejoras en las defensas de su imperio. En esta época, los conflictos con Francia se habían intensificado y las cordiales relaciones con Inglaterra habían comenzado a deteriorarse, aunque la media hermana de la reina Isabel de Inglaterra se había casado con Felipe. La reina Isabel aprobó el comercio ilegal, promoviendo así la carrera de corsarios ingleses, cuyas incursiones en el Caribe son tan famosas. La actividad de los corsarios era una empresa conjunta respaldada por los inversionistas ingleses y la nobleza. Todos compartieron las ganancias de un viaje exitoso. De esta forma, muchos centros españoles de riqueza y transporte en América eran presa de un creciente número de corsarios.

Los reyes de España conocieron bien a la familia Antonelli. Era una dinastía de ingenieros civiles y militares que ya habían diseñado defensas e instrumentos de asedio en Rusia y Hungría contra las invasiones de los otomanos. También Juan Bautista se había convertido en un destacado profesional. La primera misión encomendada a Antonelli fue la fortificación del estrecho de Magallanes, pero por razones que probablemente nunca se sabrán, el capitán general Diego Flores de Valdés, comandante de la expedición, saboteó la expedición. El ingeniero tuvo suerte de regresar con vida a España. Los buenos oficios de un amigo impidieron que el nombre de Antonelli se viera envuelto en el desastre del estrecho, asegurándole un nuevo encargo real. Aunque debilitado por problemas de salud y frecuentes conflictos con funcionarios coloniales, esta nueva misión inició la fase culminante de su carrera como arquitecto militar.

Primero fue a Cartagena, la ciudad que había vivido muchos años de conflictos con los piratas. Antonelli diseñó un plan para aprovechar la capacidad defensiva del lugar. Le pareció obvio que el bloqueo y la fortificación de las entradas naturalmente angostas de la bahía resultarían mucho más eficaces para impedir una invasión que los terraplenes tan fácilmente superados por Drake. Sus asistentes también construyeron fuertes temporarios y se iniciaron los trabajos de un plan permanente de defensa con tres masivas fortalezas.

Antonelli también pasó tiempo en Cuba y en Panamá. En mil quinientos ochenta y ocho el rey le encomendó convertir los planes de defensa de Cartagena en piedra y argamasa.

En mil seiscientos dieciséis, la muerte terminó su odisea de cuarenta años al servicio del rey.

(Adaptación de: "Arquitecto de las defensas del rey". *Américas*, octubre, 2003, pp. 6-15.)

Final exercise

10. Read the following sections from various newspaper articles.

a. Respecto a la situación de la tercera edad, una población cada vez más numerosa, Alberdi cree que, a pesar de la proliferación de residencias para ancianos en todas las comunidades autónomas, nuestros mayores desean estar cerca de los suyos.

b. El enemigo, por consiguiente, es caricaturizado hasta el punto de considerarlo el más malintencionado de los enemigos imaginables.

c. Los diez mandamientos son para cumplirlos, independientemente de si se tiene un ángel de la guarda al lado que le esté diciendo que hay que cumplirlos.

d. Y teniendo en cuenta que la situación económica no sólo es manifiestamente mala en las regiones, sino dentro de la propia Rusia, el problema podría ser más grave de lo que parece.

e. La financiación de la Iglesia es uno de los temas que más preocupan a los obispos españoles, que desde el pasado mes de septiembre están manteniendo conversaciones con el gobierno para conseguir una financiación estable.

f. En la operación en zonas de mantenimiento y como mecanismo de emergencia, es posible operar los trenes en el modo manual a bordo del vehículo.

g. En este sentido, es significativo el nombramiento de los cuarenta y un senadores nombrados por el Rey, que casi pueden seguir siendo considerados como "de Ayete".

h. ... porque cada máquina, cada equipo, cada producto que importábamos subía de precio, mientras el precio de nuestro azúcar, principal renglón exportable, que era el del mercado mundial, más una prima de preferencia y el de otros productos básicos, se mantenían fijos a partir de los precios alcanzados el primer año del convenio.

i. Por supuesto que, en su tiempo, se cometieron muchos abusos por las fuerzas de seguridad, pero la mayoría de víctimas eran delincuentes comunes y éstos se mantenían bajo control.

j. Los nombres que se mencionan para conformar la Comisión de la Verdad son de gente muy honorable, pero la comunidad médica está escandalizada porque alguien quiere colar a un médico que no ha pasado un préstamo con COFINA y nunca dio explicaciones sobre el uso de material médico propiedad del Estado en su clínica privada.

13

Laterals /l/ and /ʎ/

The phoneme /l/ in Spanish

The lateral phoneme /l/ and the rhotic phonemes /r/ and /ɾ/ belong to the category of liquid consonants because they are halfway in between consonants and vowels: produced with some of the characteristic sonority of vowels, but also with an obstruction (albeit a weaker one than with other consonants) between the tongue and the alveolar ridge.

The alveolar [l] has the same place of articulation as the alveolar [n] in **nene**. However, [n] is a nasal sound because the velum is lowered, which directs the air to exit through the nose rather than the mouth. For [l], there is a partial obstruction formed with the tongue tip and the alveolar ridge, while some of the air escapes on both sides of the tongue. Check the difference by touching the alveolar ridge with the tongue. Now say [n] and then [l]. Can you feel that, for the [n], the sides of your tongue curve slightly toward the roof of the mouth, and the tip of the tongue and the sides touch the alveolar ridge? This produces a complete occlusion that blocks the air from exiting through your mouth. For the [l], the tip of the tongue again touches the alveolar ridge, but the sides of the tongue are lowered, letting the air exit by circumventing the tongue on both sides of the mouth.

Just like the [n], the [l] also assimilates to the place of articulation of the following consonant, but only if it is dental, palatal or affricate. This phenomenon, as we already know, is called **ASSIMILATION**.

[l] **VOICED ALVEOLAR LATERAL**

any position, except before dental and palatal consonants: **lejos** ['le.xos], **ala** ['a.la], **costal** [kos.'tal], **alma** ['al.ma], **Carlos** ['kaɾ.los]

[l̪] **VOICED DENTAL LATERAL**

only before [t] and [d]: **alto** ['al̪.to], **caldo** ['kal̪.do]

[ʎ] **VOICED PALATAL LATERAL**

only before palatal consonants [ɟ, tʃ, ɲ]: **colchón** [koʎ.'tʃon], **el chico** [eʎ.'tʃi.ko], **el llanto** [eʎ.'ɟan.to], **el yeso** [eʎ.'ɟe.so], **el ñoño** [eʎ.'ɲo.ɲo], etc.

Remember that in Spanish, assimilation occurs no only at the word level: (e.g. **colchón** = [koʎ.'tʃon]), but also takes place accross words in phonological phrases, (e.g. **el chico** = [eʎ.›tʃi.ko], **el yeso** = [eʎ.›ɟe.so]).

In the south of Spain (especially in Andalusia), in the Caribbean, but also in Panama and Venezuela, at the end of syllables, some people pronounce the [ɾ] as if it were an [l] and vice versa. Because these are different phonemes, some people criticize this pronunciation, arguing that it could cause confusion if someone says **arma** ['ar:ma] instead of **alma** ['al.ma] and **alto** ['al:to] instead of **harto** ['aɾ.to], but in the context where the words are uttered there is usually no ambiguity. (There is more information in Chapter 17.)

The phoneme /l/ in English

The phoneme /l/ in Spanish is different from the phoneme /l/ in English. English has two variations:

[l] **VOICED ALVEOLAR LATERAL**

word-initially: `lunch` ['lʌntʃ], `let's` ['lɛts]

syllable initially: `calendar` ['kæ.lən.dɚ], `mallet` ['mæ.lət]

[ɫ] VOICED VELAR LATERAL

at the end of words and syllables: hall ['hɔɫ], smell ['smɛɫ], milk ['mɪɫk], alright [ɔɫ.ˈɹaɪt]

In American English, like in Spanish, /l/ is alveolar. The big difference is that, to produce it, the back of the tongue raises and retracts towards the velum. The space between the tongue and the velum can be so narrow that a friction is produced. At the same time, the tip of the tongue touches the alveolar ridge.

Frequently, at the end of words or syllables, for example in alright (under the influence of the following r) the American l vocalizes, meaning it becomes a vowel, with a velar place of articulation. The tongue dorsum raises towards the palate, but the tip of the tongue does not touch the alveolar ridge. This means that the l in the English words tall, triple and bill can be pronounced two ways, either with or without touching the alveolar ridge: ['tʰɔːɫ], ['tʰɹɪ.pəɫ], ['bɪɫ] but also ['tʰɔːw], ['tʰɹɪ.pəw], ['bɪw].

Let's practice

When speaking Spanish, English speakers must be aware of the difference between [l] and [ɫ]. The American [ɫ] is not part of the phonetic system of Spanish. Additionally, it can velarize the preceding vowel, causing a word like **tal** [tal] to sound like [tɔːɫ]. This pronunciation sometimes is accompanied be a lengthening of this vowel, which can also result in the production of a vowel sound that is not part of the inventory of Spanish.

The English phonological system tends to interfere in Spanish mostly when /l/ either precedes a consonant or occurs in word-final position. It is important to pay close attention to this problem and practice the articulation of /l/ in these critical positions a great deal.

The phoneme /ʎ/ in Spanish

The phoneme /ʎ/ has only one allophone:

[ʎ] VOICED PALATAL LATERAL

in various positions that correspond to the written **ll**, only in LLEÍSTA varieties of Spanish: **llamar** [ʎa.›mar], **llanta** ['ʎan.ta], **hallar** [a.'ʎar], **anillo** [a.ˈni.ʎo], etc.

There is a small number of speakers in the northeast of the Iberian Peninsula, in Castilla León, La Rioja and Cantabria, as well as in a few regions in Latin America, particularly in Paraguay and the Andes, that still distinguish the articulation of **ll** and **y**, and who pronounce **ll** as a voiced palatal lateral sound. These speakers pronounce **calle** as ['ka.ʎe] instead of ['ka.ʝe]. Sometimes, for example in the case of **vaya** ['ba.ʝa] and **valla** ['ba.ʎa], pairs of words that are homophones in most of the Spanish-speaking world continue to be pronounced distinctively in these areas. Linguists call the distinction between [ʝ] and [ʎ] and the pronunciation of **ll** as [ʎ] **LLEÍSMO**.

Exercises

1. **Read the following series of words and try to pronounce the l in the last column (with l in final position) like the l in the two words before. Read across the columns, and be careful to avoid the dark l.**

alalá	ala	al
Elena	ele	el
pelele	pelea	piel
sola	ola	sol
colilla	cola	col
Liliana	lila	mil
ensalada	sale	sal

2. **Pronounce the l in the second column the same way as in the first one, and be careful to avoid the dark l.**

calamar	calma	lanzar	alcanzar
alabar	alba	Lázaro	alcázar
alegre	álgebra	culinario	culminación
hola	Olga	colina	culmina
balón	balcón	olor	olmo
alejar	almejar	colo	colmo
baleta	almena	escalo	calmo
ala	alma	palo	palmo
ala	alba	alea	aldea
ala	alca	calor	caldo

3. **Read the following tongue twisters with the letter l.**

Qué col colosal colocó en aquel local el loco aquel.

Qué colosal col colocó el loco aquél en aquel local.

Pablito clavó un clavito. ¿Qué clavito clavó Pablito? Cabral clavó un clavo. ¿Qué clavo clavó Cabral?

La piel del jovial Manuel, siempre fiel a la ley local, luce como la miel de un panal singular.

Final exercise

4. The following sentences are taken from various newspaper articles. Read them and pay attention to the pronunciation of the letter l.

a. **Cocaleros bloquean carretera boliviana**

Unos cinco mil cocaleros protagonizaron un bloqueo de la principal ruta de Bolivia, en contra de la proyectada instalación de tres bases militares en la convulsa región del Chapare. Los productores comenzaron el bloqueo de la vía que vincula el eje troncal del país conformado por los departamentos de La Paz (oeste), Cochabamba (centro) y Santa Cruz (este).

b. **Dañan reloj solar en la ciudadela incaica de Machu Picchu en el Cuzco**

La estructura pétrea conocida como Intihuatana o reloj solar, en la célebre ciudadela incaica Machu Picchu, resultó dañada al caerle encima el brazo de una grúa mecánica, durante el rodaje de un comercial de televisión ... Su deterioro causó indignación en círculos intelectuales y culturales, que cuestionan la falta de un reglamento especial para proteger el parque arqueológico de Machu Picchu, que es Patrimonio Cultural de la Humanidad.

c. **Argentina propone al tango como patrimonio de la Humanidad**

El gobierno argentino lanzó en la UNESCO la candidatura de Tango como patrimonio oral e intangible de la Humanidad. La presentación consistió en un trabajo de investigación con material producido por las academias nacionales de tango de Argentina y Uruguay. El expediente contiene copias de partituras originales de temas famosos, libros de colecciones y un CD multimedia con música, biografías y películas.

14

The phonological phrase and the linking of words

In the dictionary, words represent the largest units of meaning. When we speak or write, however, the more relevant units of meaning are phrases or sentences. All the words between two pauses or periods of silence in speech, or between punctuation marks (period, comma, semicolon, question marks, etc.) in writing, create a **PHONOLOGICAL PHRASE**. We do not pause after each word when we speak; instead we try to group them into larger chunks according to certain semantic, logical, rhetorical, and other criteria, almost as if they were extremely long words. There is no universal rule that tells us how many words we can combine between two periods of silence; it depends on many factors, for example our lung capacity, whether we are speaking slowly or rapidly, whether we are speaking spontaneously or reading from a script, whether we are familiar with a text we are reading, etc. Periods and commas in a text show us where we should normally pause to breathe, but sometimes we must pause before because we are out of breath and have to find another spot.

Linking between consonants and vowels

Witin a phonological phrase, a consonant at the end of a word is always linked to the vowel that begins the next word. The most frequent combinations are **d, l, n, r, s** + vowels. The phrase **al entrar en el edificio**, for example, is pronounced **a-len-tra-re-ne-le-di-fi-cio**; **jugar al ajedrez, ju-ga-ra-la-je-drez**; **las águilas en el aire, la-sá-gui-la-se-ne-lai-re**; **un árbol en España, u-nár-bo-le-nes-pa-ña**, etc. As you can see, the entire phonological phrase [a.len̪.tra.re.ne.le.ði.fi.sjo] is treated as if it were a word and the same rules are applied that were explained in Chapter 3:

1. A rhythmic unit has at least one vowel.

2. When vowels and consonants alternate (... VCVCV ...), syllables are divided AFTER the vowel and BEFORE the consonant (... V-CV-CV ...). The consonant starts the syllable: **dos anillos elaborados** = do-sa-ni-llo-se-la-bo-ra-dos etc. As you can see, all the syllables in the previous example, except for the last one, are open syllables, which means that they end in a vowel. This type of syllable is preferred in Spanish and is the most frequent. The last consonant of the phrase forms the coda of the final syllable.

3. Consonant clusters **p, t, c, b, d, g, f** + **l** or **r**, are not divided: **ciudad rusa** = ciu-da-**dru**-sa, **kétchup rojo** = két-chu-**pro**-jo. There are not many words that end in **p, t, c, b, g** or **f**. The only frequent word-final consonant in Spanish that can create a complex onset is **d**.

   Two identical consonants are fused and become one sound: **el libro** [e.'li.βro], **en Navarra** [e.na.'βa.ra].

Vowel fusion and adjustments accross words

When a vowel at the end of a word meets another at the beginning of the next word, three fairly predictable things can happen:

When a high vowel (**u** or **i**) in an unstressed syllable is adjacent to a mid or low vowel (**a, e, o**), the result is a diphthong, for example in **la unión** [aw], **mi amigo** [ja], **la tribu amazónica** [wa]. This is also called **SYNALEPHA**, because the creation of a diphthong results in fewer syllables. Look at the box below. If you speak slowly, it is possible to articulate both vowels separately, as if they were pure vowels (column SLOW). However, you should not separate the two vowels with a **GLOTTAL STOP**, which is a complete closure of the vocal cords, that cuts the first vocal sound off and blocks the flow of air. When you open the **GLOTTIS** for the second vowel, a small explosion is produced that starts with an abrupt vocalic onset. If you talk at a normal speed or fast, the two vowels are articulated as diphthongs (column NORMAL/ FAST).

	SLOW	NORMAL/ FAST
mi amor	[mi.a.'mor]	[mja.'mor]
mi era	[mi.'e.ra]	['mje.ra]
y Ana	[i.'a.na]	['ja.na]
y ojo	[i.'o.xo]	['jo.xo]
tu amor	[tu.a.'mor]	[twa.'mor]
tu era	[tu.'e.ra]	['twe.ra]
tu ojo	[tu.'o.xo]	['two.xo]
tu hija	[tu.'i.xa]	['twi.xa]*

*There is dialectal and other variation when it comes to the pronunciation of unstressed **u** and **i**. Normally the outcome is a rising diphthong: **tu imágen** [twi.'ma.xen], however, you may also hear a falling diphthong [tuj.'ma.xen].

The mid back **o** in stressed syllables together with **a**, **e**, **í**, **ú** can also be reduced to the semivowel [w] in informal or very rapid speech:

	SLOW	NORMAL/ FAST
O es Juan	[o.es.'xwan]	[wes.'xwan]
O Ana	[o.'a.na]	['wa.na]
sigo asi	['si.ɣo.a.'si]	['si.ɣwa.'si]

When two adjacent vowels occur in stressed syllables, the result is a **HIATUS** (TWO SYLLABLES):e.g. **era una** [e.ra'u.na]; **la era** [la.'e.ra]; **la hora** [la.'o.ra]; **fue otro** ['fwe.'o.t̪ro]; **fue Ana** ['fwe.'ana]; **e India** [e.'in.ðja]; té único ['te.'u.ni.ko].

When two of the same unstressed vowels occur adjacent to one another, they are reduced to one unstressed vowel: **est<u>e e</u>dificio** ['es.**te**. ði.'fi.sjo], **l<u>a A</u>lhambra** [**la**.'lam.bra]. This is very different from English, where adjacent same vowels are separated with a glottal stop.

In Spanish, when the FIRST vowel is stressed, the result is a stressed vowel as well: **fu<u>e E</u>lena** ['f**we**.'le.na]. If the SECOND or BOTH are stressed, the result is a lengthened vowel. (In a phonetic transcription this is indicated with a colon (:) [a:, e:, i:, o:, u:].): **habl<u>a á</u>rabe** ['a.'β**la:**.ra.βe] or **habr<u>á á</u>guilas** [a.'β**ra:**.ɣi.las].

V + V → V **este edificio** ['es.te.ɗi.'fi.sjo]

V́ + V → V́ **fue Elena** ['fwe.'le.na]

V + V́ → V́: **habla árabe** ['a.'βla:.ɾa.βe]

V́ + V́ → V́: **habrá águilas** [a.'βɾa:.ɣi.las]

The same rule applies for three vowels of the same kind together, for example in **va a hablar** [ba:.'βlaɾ] or **lee eso** ['le:.so].

The linking of words produces the typical rhythm of spoken Spanish, characterized by the dominance of open syllables (those ending in vowels). This linking makes it difficult for foreigners to detect individual words and therefore to understand utterances, and gives the impression that the Spanish language is spoken very rapidly.

Exercises

1. **Read the following sentences slowly and pay attention to the linking of words. In this exercise, use slashes (/) to show where syllables begin. Circle the hiatuses and the fusion of vowels between words.**

   a. Eso no se le olvida a nadie. Pero ya tendría él que estar aquí. Mi último recuerdo de su esposa fue el de una noche de grandes lluvias.

   b. En ella la exorcizó una hechicera.

   c. No era una bruja convencional sino una mujer simpática.

   d. Con el último esfuerzo que hizo.

   e. Él habla hasta su última hora.

   f. Como a última hora no encontramos a nadie.

   g. ...y en menos de media hora habíamos llegado a una conclusión.

   h. ...y el mismo día y a la misma hora en que puse el punto final a estas memorias.

2. **Now do the same exercise again but read the sentences more rapidly.**

3. **Do the same with the following sentences taken from Colombian newspapers.**

   a. La última vez que un gobierno se vio obligado a aplicar la dictadura fiscal fue en mil novecientos ochenta y siete.

   b. En esa ocasión, el proyecto no pasó en las cámaras legislativas por la oposición que le hizo el Partido Conservador al gobierno de ese momento.

   c. Sin embargo, a la hora de observar la participación sobre el total, el crecimiento no es grande.

d. El saldo en rojo de este año ya va en más de veinte millones de pesos.

e. El club acogió el puerto cundimarqués como sede y esta es la hora en que nadie ha respondido a las expectativas.

f. Ese dinero corresponde a la diferencia entre lo que le cuesta a un exportador comprar el café en el país y lo que recibe a la hora de cambiar por pesos los dólares que le pagan por cada saco.

g. Numerosas atenciones se han ofrecido en honor de Elena Hosie Acevedo.

h. Su voz es bastante melodiosa que se ajusta a los temas con el suave ritmo antillano, con la estructura balada básica o con deliciosos interludios de saxo que le dan ese saborcito a jazz que presenta en algunas canciones.

i. Está ubicado en una de las zonas más costosas del mundo, a unos pasos del área hotelera más cara de Nueva York.

j. Fabio Parra se encuentra en el otro extremo.

4. Finally, do the same exercise with the following text about Colombia.

COLOMBIA

La República de Colombia está ubicada en el noroeste de Sudamérica, limita al norte con Panamá y el mar Caribe, al este con Venezuela y Brasil, al sur con Perú y Ecuador, y al oeste con el océano Pacífico. Colombia es el único país de América del Sur con costas tanto en el océano Atlántico como en el océano Pacífico.

El elemento topográfico más característico de Colombia es la cordillera de los Andes, situada en la parte central y occidental del país, que se extiende de norte a sur a través de casi toda su longitud.

Colombia es el primer exportador mundial de esmeraldas y tiene otras reservas minerales considerables. El café es el cultivo principal. Después de Brasil, Colombia es el segundo productor mundial y el primero en la producción de café suave. Otras industrias destacadas son las dedicadas a la elaboración de alimentos, productos de tabaco, hierro y acero, y equipos de transporte, así como la industria editorial. Los productos químicos están adquiriendo un auge creciente, así como el calzado, la industria textil y la petrolífera.

El idioma oficial es el español, pero se hablan más de sesenta lenguas indígenas, que provienen de varias familias lingüísticas.

15

Rhythm in the phonological phrase

Each phonological phrase in Spanish has its own specific rhythm which is characterized by **STRESS** (Span. **ACENTO PROSÓDICO** o **DE INTENSIDAD**.

We already know that, at the word level, the nucleus of a syllable is a vowel and that there is only one stressed syllable in each Spanish word while all the others are unstressed (See Chapter 3). All syllables in Spanish have more or less the same duration, which means that the duration of a sentence or phrase depends on the number of syllables in it. We call this **SYLLABLE TIMING**.

The rhythm in English

In English, some syllables have a stronger degree of stress than others. Syllables with primary stress are the longest, followed by those with secondary stress, and finally, unstressed syllables which can be significantly shorter. There is an approximately equal amount of time between stressed syllables. Consequently, the duration of a sentence or phrase is predominantly based on the number of syllables with primary stress that comprise it. We call this **STRESS TIMING**. The stress pattern in the English word `responsibility`, for example, can be characterized as follows:

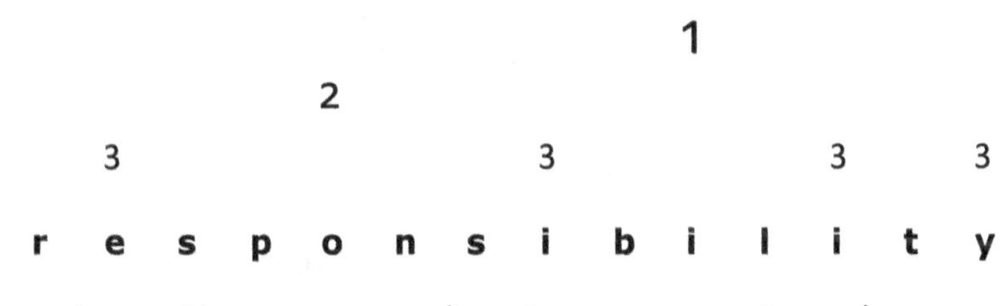

The 'schwa' sound [ə] in English

In English, vowels in unstressed syllables are much shorter than those in stressed syllables. Many are reduced or relaxed such that they are produced with a neutral tongue position resulting in a mid central vowel, [ə]. The name for this sound is **SCHWA**, and in the word `responsibility` above, it is the sound of the unstressed vowels represented by the letter **i**. All of the letters that represent vowels, when they are not stressed, can be pronounced [ə], for example in `another`, `taken`, `university`, `political`, `minute`, etc. This sound does not exist in Spanish and it is important to avoid it.

Rhythm in Spanish

In Spanish, things are much easier: syllables are either stressed or not; there is no secondary stress. All vowels have roughly the same length and duration, though there are minor differences between the different vowels. In the word Atacama, for example, there are four (4) [a] sounds, pronounced the same way, and only one is stressed. The duration of the stressed a is slightly longer, but not noticeably so without measuring it, and it is also characterized by a higher pitch and greater articulatory effort.

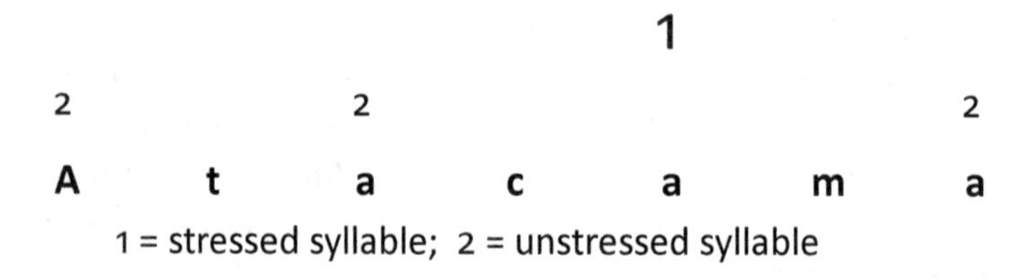

1 = stressed syllable; 2 = unstressed syllable

Because there is no secondary stress in Spanish, it may sound a bit flat to English speakers, who often naturally apply English stress patterns to Spanish, but in order to master Spanish pronunciation, it is important to avoid vowel reduction and secondary stress.

Not every word in a phonetic phrase has a stressed syllable in Spanish, but it somewhat straightforward to determine which words are stressed. Words with lexical meaning, i.e. those that convey obvious descriptive content are stressed. Most NOUNS and their modifiers, which means ADJECTIVES: **casa *blanca***; VERBS and their modifiers, ADVERBS: **fuimos *ayer***; QUESTION WORDS: **¿quién?**; SUBJECT PRO-

NOUNS: **usted**; PREPOSITIONAL PRONOUNS: **cerca de *ti***; the LONG FORMS OF POSSESSIVES: **tuyo**, **suyo**; OTHER WORDS THAT CARRY MEANING como **sí**, **no**, etc.

Functional or "grammatical" words, which indicate grammatical relationships and provide structure to the language, are generally unstressed. These include ARTICLES: ***el*** **perro**, the SHORT FORMS OF POSSESSIVES: *mi* **padre**; DIRECT AND INDIRECT OBJECT PRONOUNS: ***se lo*** **dimos**; the verbs **ser** and **estar** when they are auxiliary verbs: **La carta *fue* escrita por el presidente. Mi padre está hablando con la profesora**; PREPOSITIONS: ***de*** **mí**, ***por*** **ti**, ***con*** **él**; **no** when it means not: **No, *no* lo llamé**; etc.

"Jabberwocky," a nonsense poem that appears in Lewis Carroll's *Through the Looking-Glass*, contains numerous invented words that resemble English but are unintelligible. Although the meaning escaped Alice, the poem is instructive for us because throughout, the grammatical words (and affixes) provide the context that allows for identification of the various parts of speech of adjacent words.

> T'was brillig, and the slithy toves/ Did gyre and gimble in the wabe: / All mimsy were the borogoves,/ And the mome raths outgrabe.

T'was indicates that an adjective or –ing form of a verb follows. Here there is no –ing, so it is either an adjective or an adverb. In the slithy toves English word order requires that the adjective precede the noun in this circumstance, and the –y ending provides an additional clue that it is an adjective. All is an intensifier, showing that an adjective or an adverb follows (here it has to be an adjective). The the before borogoves indicates that borogoves is a (plural) noun, and so on. All the grammatical words here are unstressed, while the lexical words that provide meaning (even if we cannot understand that meaning) are stressed.

Exercises

1. **Read the following sentences taken from various sources, mark the stressed syllables, and pay special attention to the pronunciation of words that are cognates.**

a. Tras dos días de intensos debates, salpicados de animosidad y resentimiento, el congreso socialdemócrata aprobó, por doscientos sesenta y ocho votos contra veintiocho, la fusión con los liberales.

b. Razón de sobra para que ninguna ley pueda ser objeto de "interpretaciones subjetivas", pues con ello se abre una vía franca para el autoritarismo, el despotismo y la arbitrariedad.

c. El sistema garantiza todas las necesidades de seguridad relacionadas con el cifrado de documentos, la autenticidad de los intervinientes y la certificación del contenido o la fecha de emisión de los correspondientes documentos.

d. Sigamos con el tema del placer. Desde el ángulo de la bioelectricidad, cuanto más abrupta sea la caída de potencial, mayor es la sensación de placer.

e. Según los datos del Parlamento de Quito, la medida propuesta por el gobierno español supondría el regreso de entre ciento cincuenta mil y doscientos mil súbditos ecuatorianos, que en la actualidad viven y trabajan en la clandestinidad en España.

f. Según los priístas, debe haber compatibilidad entre los programas de Operación Política y el de Elecciones, por lo que pondrán especial énfasis en la organización de mujeres, jóvenes, diputados, organización electoral y líderes sociales.

g. El tiempo mínimo de disponibilidad de ambulancia es de cinco minutos y el máximo de sesenta minutos.

h. ¡Remedios, mujer! Estoy hablando en general. España va muy retrasada con respecto a la nueva espiritualidad del mundo y así seguirá mientras a los maestros no se les eleve a la categoría moral que les corresponde, mientras no se les dé el rango social que se merecen.

i. Hablar para arriba, o sólo desde arriba, favorece la generalización, la frustración y la incredibilidad.

j. Lo significativo de la cuestión fiscal hay que buscarlo más bien en la vulnerabilidad que incorpora en las finanzas públicas la dependencia de éstas respecto al capital financiero nacional e internacional.

k. En África, sin ir más lejos, existen grandes potencialidades para la generación de hidroelectricidad, pero su localización las mantiene aún, y quizá por mucho tiempo, inexplotadas.

2. **Read the following article and determine which words receive phrasal-level stress, and mark the corresponding stressed syllable in those words.**

El desierto de Atacama

Una quinta parte de la superficie terrestre está ocupada por desiertos. Pero pocos de ellos concuerdan con la imagen tópica de un mar de dunas que se desplazan a merced de los vientos.

En el desierto chileno de Atacama las erupciones del volcán Parinacota causaron la emergencia de lagos en cuyas riberas crecen unas extrañas vegetaciones adaptadas a las condiciones brumosas, además de grandes lagos salados y géiseres a cuatro mil trescientos veintiún metros de altitud.

Habitado por pueblos indígenas herederos de las extinguidas camanchacas, proanches y atacameños, los aymaras del altiplano han asimilado un modo de vida basado en la cría de llamas y alpacas y el cultivo de maíz y patata.

Este espacio extremo, acaso el más árido del planeta, ofrece oportunidades para la práctica de deportes de aventura, senderismo y rutas a caballo entre los volcanes más altos del Cono Sur.

16
Intonation

Because it affects the meaning and interpretation of an utterance, intonation is a very important aspect of pronunciation. In Chapter 15 we discussed another **suprasegmental** aspect of language, the rhythm of an utterance, or in other words, the combination of stressed and unstressed syllables in the speech chain, as well as syllable duration and the links between words. Intonation refers to the frequency with which a speaker's vocal cords vibrate when speaking, the auditory counterpart of which is **PITCH.**

In **AUTOSEGMENTAL-METRICAL THEORY** of phonology, it is assumed that there are two abstract levels in which various components of speech reside. The segmental level contains the segments—vowels and consonants—that combine in different ways to form syllables, while the **SUPRASEGMENTAL** level contains the characteristics of speech that accompany segments, like rhythm, stress, and intonation.

Syllables, made of consonants and vowels, belong to the segmental level, and intonation exists on a distinct level. However, they are not totally independent of each other, because they are linked at certain key points: stressed syllables, and utterance boundaries. The tone or sequence of tones associated with a stressed syllables is called a **PITCH ACCENT**, and that associated with a boundary is called a **BOUNDARY TONE**. So if we think about stressed syllables and boundaries as anchors for pitch, the contour between anchors can be understood as interpolation or transition between for example, the pitch accent associated with one stressed syllable to the pitch accent associated with the next stressed syllable. This is shown in the image below. In the utterance **Mi amiga es de Argentina**, there are anchors for the pitch on the two stressed syllables, *-mi-* and *-ti-*, as well as another anchor at the right boundary, associated with the last syllable, *-na*.

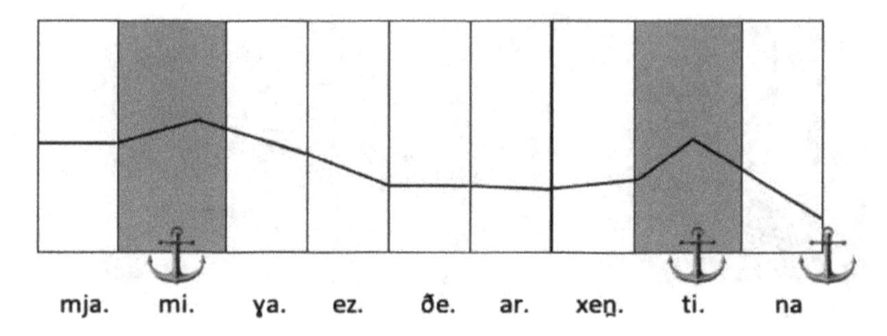

There have been several different models to represent and describe intonational contours and their relation to the segmental level. Here we use the ToBI (Tone and Break Indices) system, which uses various combinations of "H", "L", and "*" to represent pitch accents. In this notation, H represents a high tone or "peak", L a low tone or "valley". For boundary tones, "%" is used to indicate the link with the end of phrase. The illustration below shows a schematic of the tones and nomenclature used to describe this pattern.

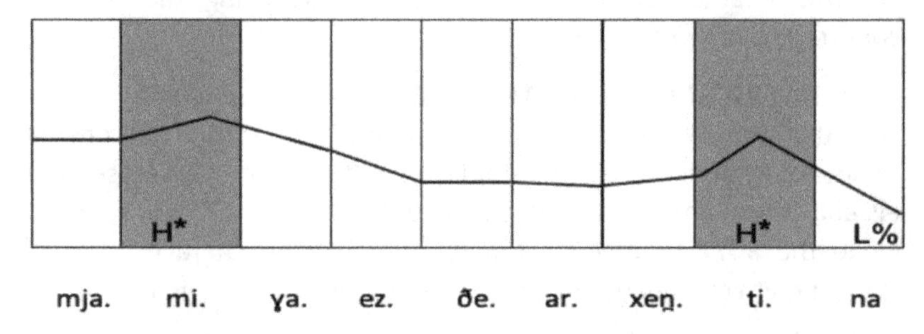

In any utterance, of all the pitch accents associated with stressed syllables, the **NUCLEAR ACCENT** is the most important. The nucleus of an utterance is the strongest prosodic position and is usually located on the last stressed syllable of an utterance, unless there is contrastive focus (the presentation and highlighting of information that contrasts with the expectations of the interlocutor). For example, if a speaker says to another "Did you say you want a lemon?", and the other speaker answers "No, I said I want a CARTON."

The criteria used to label utterances in accordance with ToBI conventions requires some explanation. Table 1 contains a description of each pitch accent used in the labelling of pitch contours and an illustration of the prototypical appearance of the contour. Table 2 shows the same information for boundary tones.

	H*	A peak: a high tone aligned within the stressed syllable without a preceding valley.
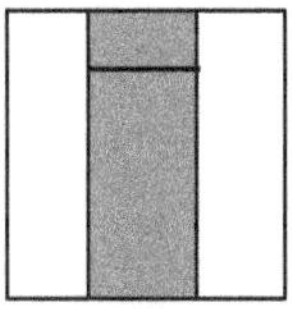	L*	A valley: a low tone realized close to the bottom of the speaker's range.
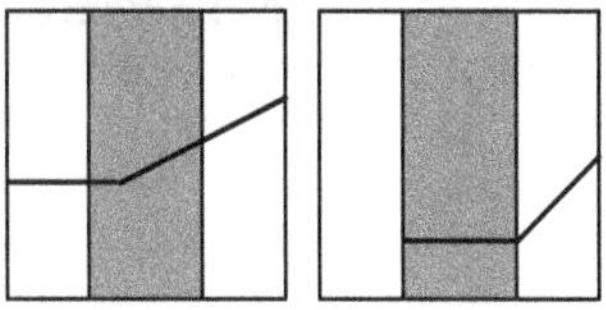	L*+H	A valley in the stressed syllable that rises toward a peak either within the post-tonic syllable or after it.
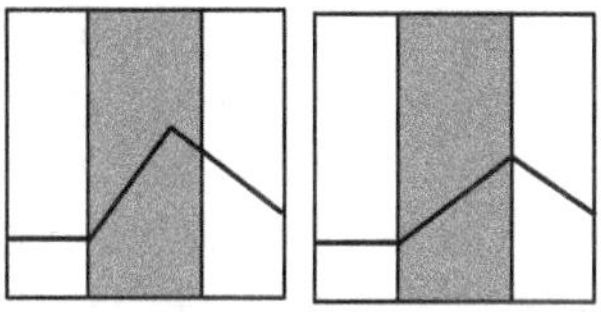	L+H*	A peak in the stressed syllable preceded by a low tone that begins to rise from the pretonic syllable.
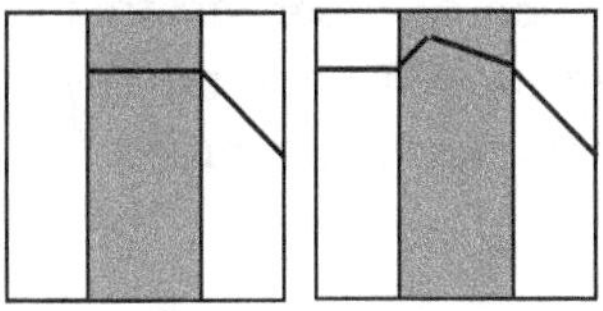	H*+L	A falling tone, descending from a peak in the stressed syllable toward a valley in the post-tonic syllable.
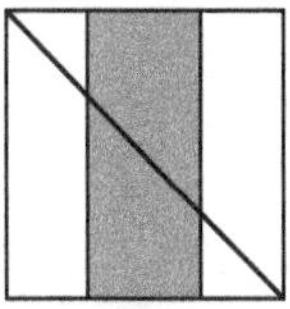	H+L*	A tone that falls throughout the stressed syllable toward a valley in or near the boundary between the stressed syllable and the post-tonic syllable.
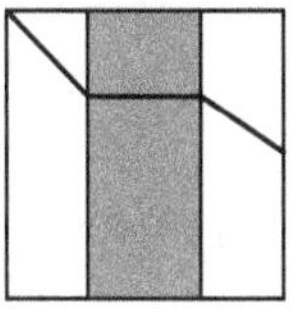	H+!H*	A falling contour that levels off in the stressed syllable, and continues to fall in the ppst-tonic syllable.

Schematic representation of pitch accents

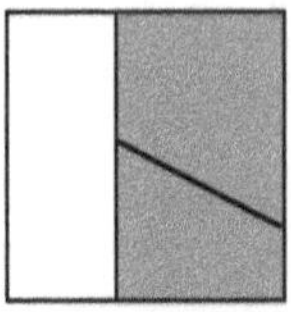	L%	A fall toward the bottom of the speaker's pitch range after the nuclear stressed syllable until the end of the utterance.
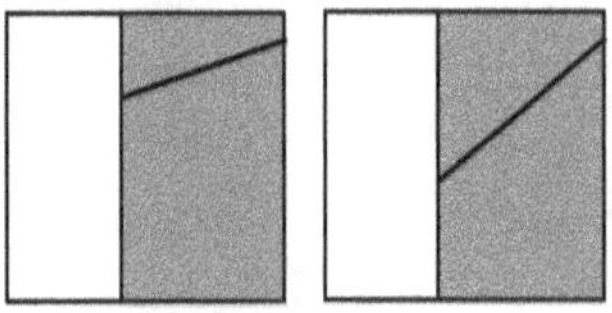	H%	A rise after the nuclear stressed syllable until the end of the utterance.
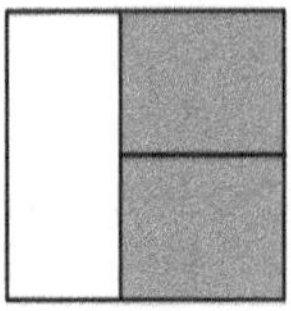	M%	A fall to an intermediate level plane from a peak in the nuclear pitch accent, or a sustained mid tone.

Schematic representation of boundary tones

Now that the labeling system has been explained, it is possible to visualize and describe the patterns employed to express different types of utterances.

Broad-focus statement

This type of utterance is a simple declaration or assertion that affirms new information or updates the conversation in a neutral way, without expressing a reaction to the information being expressed. Some examples are:

- (as a response to the question **¿Quién lo hizo?** / `Who did it?` **Juan lo hizo.** / `Juan did it.`
- (as a response to the question **¿Quién lo hizo?** / `Who did it?` **Tu padre lo hizo.** / `Your father did it.`
- (as a response to the question **¿Quién lo hizo?** / `Who did it?)` **Mi hermano lo hizo.** / `My brother did it.`
- (as a response to the question **¿Quién se lo hizo?** `Who explained it to you?)` **El otro profesor nos lo explicó.**/ `The other professor explained it to us.`
- (as a response to the question **¿Qué hace el niño?** / `What is the child doing?` **El niño juega bajo los árboles.** / `The child is playing under the trees.`

To express a neutral (broad focus) statement, in most varieties of Spanish, speakers use a nuclear contour characterized by a low or descending pitch accent to a low boundary tone. In Figure 1, we see a low pitch accent (L*) associated with the last stressed syllable of the urance, followed by a low boundary tone (L%) associated with the right edge of the utterance.

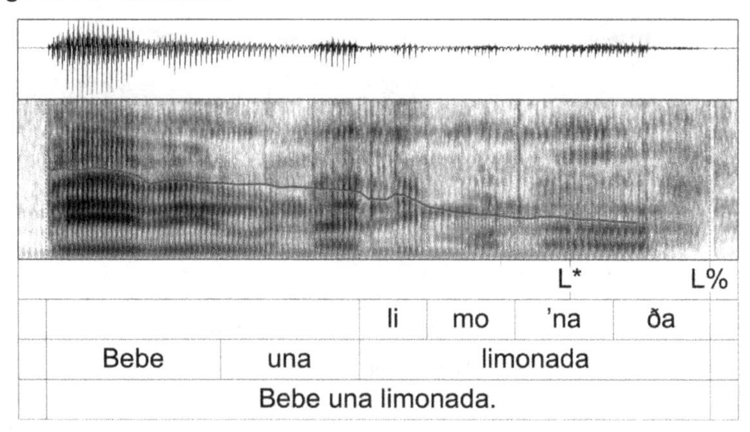

Figure 1: Bebe una limonada. (She is drinking a lemonade.)

There are exceptions to this pattern as well. The contour for this type of utterance in Dominican Spanish is more likely to show a tone that falls throughout the nuclear stressed syllable, followed by a high boundary tone, H%. In the Spanish spoken in the Andean region of Venezuela, the contour consists of a nuclear pitch accent that is high, but downstepped, or scaled lower relative to the preceding high tone, represented by "!". This tonal scaling results in a high tone that is noticeably lower than a previous peak, represented by !H*. The boundary tone in this variety remains low, L%.

Narrow focus statement

A narrow focus statement is one that highlights a word or phrase for pragmatic reasons, among them clarification or insistence. For example, if I know that I am going to give a document to David and my colleague asks me `Will you give it to Carlos?`, my answer will highlight the name `David`, in order to indicate that the answer goes against my colleague's expectation: `No, I'm going to give it to DAVID.`

In most varieties of Spanish, this type of utterance is characterized by a rising nuclear pitch accent, followed by a low boundary tone, represented as L+H* L%. In the example shown in Figure 2, the phrase **No, de limones** (`No, of lemons`) is an answer to the question **¿Un kilo de naranjas?** (`A kilo of oranges` from an interlocutor who has misunderstood the initial request. This speaker has highlighted the word limones (lemons) to clarify the misunderstanding.

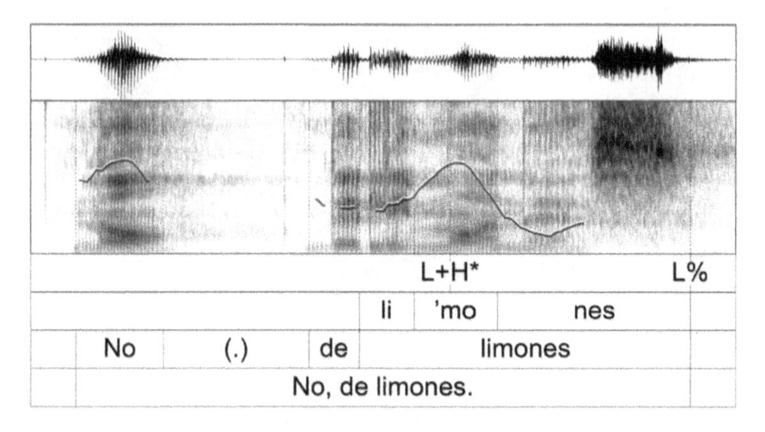

Figure 2. No, de limones. (No, of lemons)

Absolute questions

An absolute question is one that can be answered with yes or no, e.g. Do you speak English?

For this type of utterance, there is a good deal of dialectal variation in the intonational contours used. There are some dialects in which the tone rises at the end of a yes/no question, and others that show a falling pattern. For example, in Chile and in the Andean regions of Ecuador and Peru, questions of this type tend to end with a nuclear contour characterized by a high rise, usually after a valley on the nuclear stressed syllable, labeled L* HH%. Mexican Spanish is characterized a similar but slightly different contour, in which the final rise is less extreme, labeled L* LH%. However in the Andean region of Venezuela, the Canary Islands, Argentina, and the Caribbean, these questions typically show a falling contour. Figure 3 shows an example of the more common rising contour in a question from an Andean Spanish speaker in Peru asking if his interlocutor has marmalade or jam.

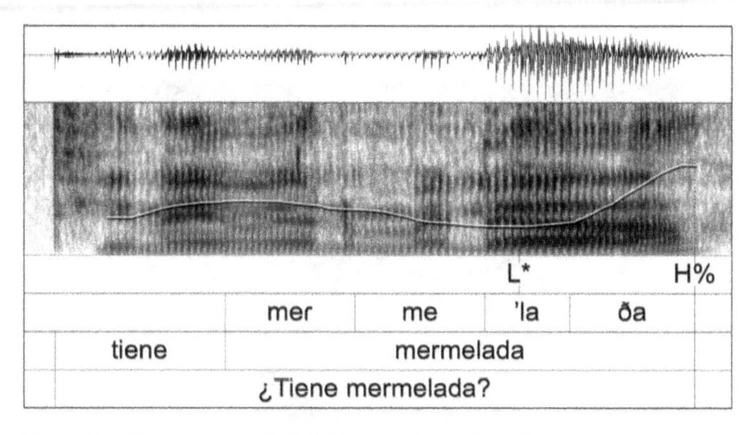

Figure 3. ¿Tiene mermelada? (Do you have jam?)

Wh- questions

A wh- question, also referred to as a pronominal question is one that contains an interrogative pronoun like What? Who? Where? When? How? or Why?. In most varieties of Spanish, this type of question is characterized by a low or falling boundary tone. There is more variation in the nuclear pitch accent, but in some varieties the same nuclear accent as used for a broad focus statement. One can speculate that it is possible to use the same contours for these two types of utterances, because the presence of the interrogative pronoun in wh-questions makes the use of distinct intonational contours as a cue to distinguish it from a broad focus statement unnecessary. Some example of these types of questions are:

- Where is the classroom?
- Who did you go to the party with?
- Why do you study phonetics?
- How is the recipe prepared?

Figure 4 shows an example of the contour used in the question **¿Qué hora es?** / What time is it? in Andean Peruvian Spanish.

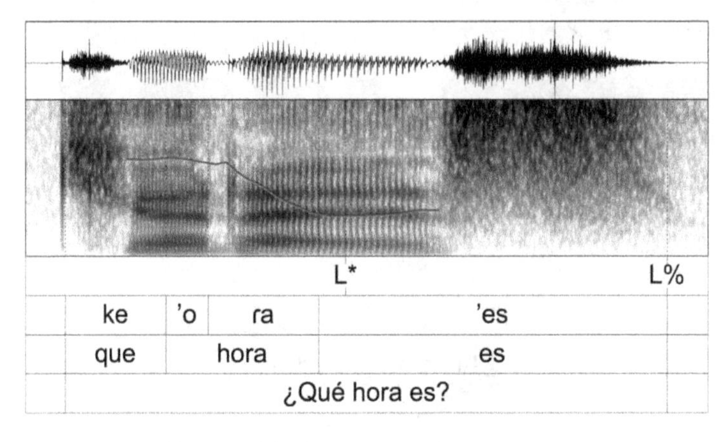

Figure 4. ¿Qué hora es? (What time is it?)

Echo wh-questions

This type of question repeats what an interlocutor has just asked, without adding additional information. It often expresses the reaction of the speaker to the question they have just heard, such as surprise, anger, sarcasm, or simply that they have not heard or understood the question. It is common for echo questions to begin with the unstressed conjunction que. The following situation illustrates an example of this: There is a fire in a classroom and all the students are outside of the room. When the professor arrives and asks them **¿Por qué no están en la sala de clase?** / `Why aren't you in the classroom?`, the incredulous students answer **¿Que por qué no estamos en la sala de clase?** / `(What do you mean) Why aren't we in the classroom?` Another example illustrating a simple repetition of a question by a speaker who wants to ensure they have understood it correctly, is: You are asked where you are going, but the room is very noisy and you are unsure if you heard correctly, so you repeat **¿Adónde voy?**/ `Where am I going?` Figure 5 shows an example of this sentence, with a marked rise at the end.

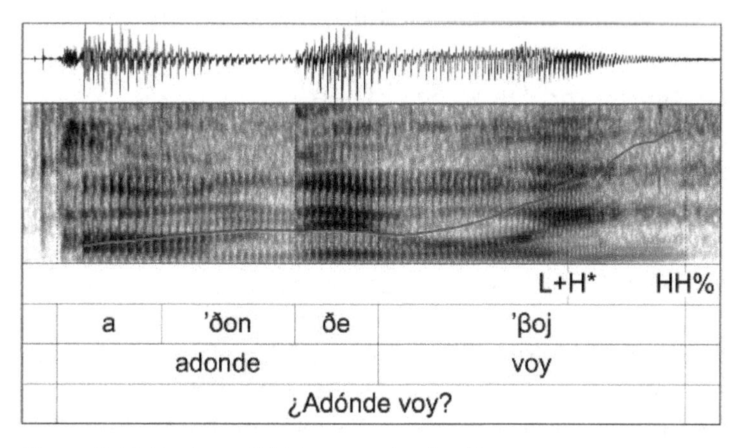

Figure 5.¿Adónde voy? (Where am I going?)

Exclamations and imperatives

In most varieties of Spanish, the nuclear contour used for exclamations is the same as that used for narrow focus statements, i.e. a rise-fall pattern, labelled L+H* L%. Imperatives in all dialects nearly always end in a low boundary tone, L%. Figure 6 shows an example of a speaker ordering a group of children to quiet down.

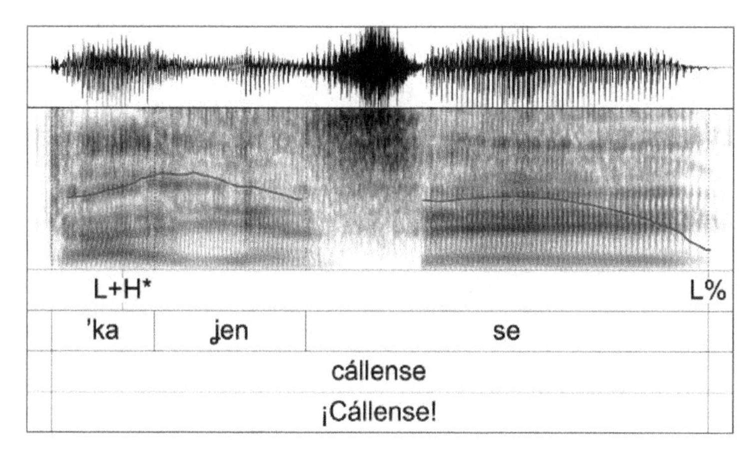

Figure 6.¡Cállense! (Be quiet!)

Other examples of exclamations that would show similar contours are:

- **¡Qué horror!** / `How terrible!`
- **¡Ven conmigo!** / `Come with me!`
- **¡Ven acá!** / `Come here!`

In addition to the aforementioned utterance types, there are others that show distinct meanings: emphatic or narrow-focus questions, utterances with multiple phonological phrases, such as multiple choice questions or lists. These show considerable dialectal variation and it is not possible to describe them all here, but we hope to have provided an introduction to the topic of intonation in Spanish, and the rich dialectal variety found throughout the Spanish-speaking world.

17
Variation

Regional pronunciation differences and other types of variation

As has been discussed throughout this book, there is considerable regional variation in the pronunciation of Spanish. This chapter presents a summary of the most common and most well-studied variation, but there are many more cases of phonetic/phonological variation, so many that it would be impossible to describe all of them here. Our hope is that this chapter will inspire you to notice and seek further information about the endless number of personal and collective articulatory differences that exist in Spanish.

In the English-speaking world, the difference in accents is often perceived in the pronunciation of vowels — a speaker from England would likely pronounce the a in bath with the same vowel as the one used in father, whereas a North American English speaker would likely use the a in cat. In contrast, in Spanish, the pronunciation of consonants is much more likely to vary regionally, while vowels remain relatively stable (although there are several cases of variation in vowel pronunciations as well). It is possible to guess where a speaker is from by noting certain aspects of their pronunciation. For example, if a new friend introduces herself saying ['ʃo.me.'ʃa.mo.'law.ra] (Yo me llamo Laura / My name is Laura), you will know by her use of the [ʃ] sound (SHEÍSMO) that she is from the Southern Cone, and more specifically, from the Rio de la Plata region. In this way, you may deduce that that your new friend probably comes from Argentina or Uruguay, without her telling you as much.

■ Distinción, seseo and ceceo

One of the main differences between Castilian Spanish (the variety spoken in the center-north of Spain) and varieties spoken in Andalusia, the Canary Islands and Latin America is the way in which they pronounce orthographic c and z. Castilian Spanish speakers use DISTINCTION, a phonemic distinction between /s/ and /θ/ such that casa is pronounced ['ka.sa] and caza as ['ka. θa].

In parts of southern Spain, the Canary Islands, and all of Latin America, speakers use /s/ for orthographic s as well as c/z. This lack of phonemic distinction is called SESEO. To use the same examples as above, in seseante dialects, both casa and caza are pronounced ['ka.sa].

The use of /θ/ not only for orthographic c and z but also for orthographic s is called CECEO, and is more geographically restricted regional phenomenon, occurring in the southernmost regions of Andalusia, as well as (albeit less frequently) in Puerto Rico and Central America. Returning to the same examples, ceceante speakers pronounce both casa and caza as ['ka. θa].

■ Variation in the pronunciation of /s/

▶ Apical s [s̺]

We saw in Chapter 9 that in Castilian Spanish (central-northern Spain) an apical pronunciation of /s/ is fairly common, while speakers of other dialects tend toward a pre-dorsal pronunciation. The difference here is the part of the tongue (the tip versus the blade) that forms the partial obstruction with the alveolar ridge. The apical pronunciation is more sibilant, meaning that more energy is concentrated in the higher resonant frequencies, and for this reason, these productions of /s/ may be perceived as more prominent.

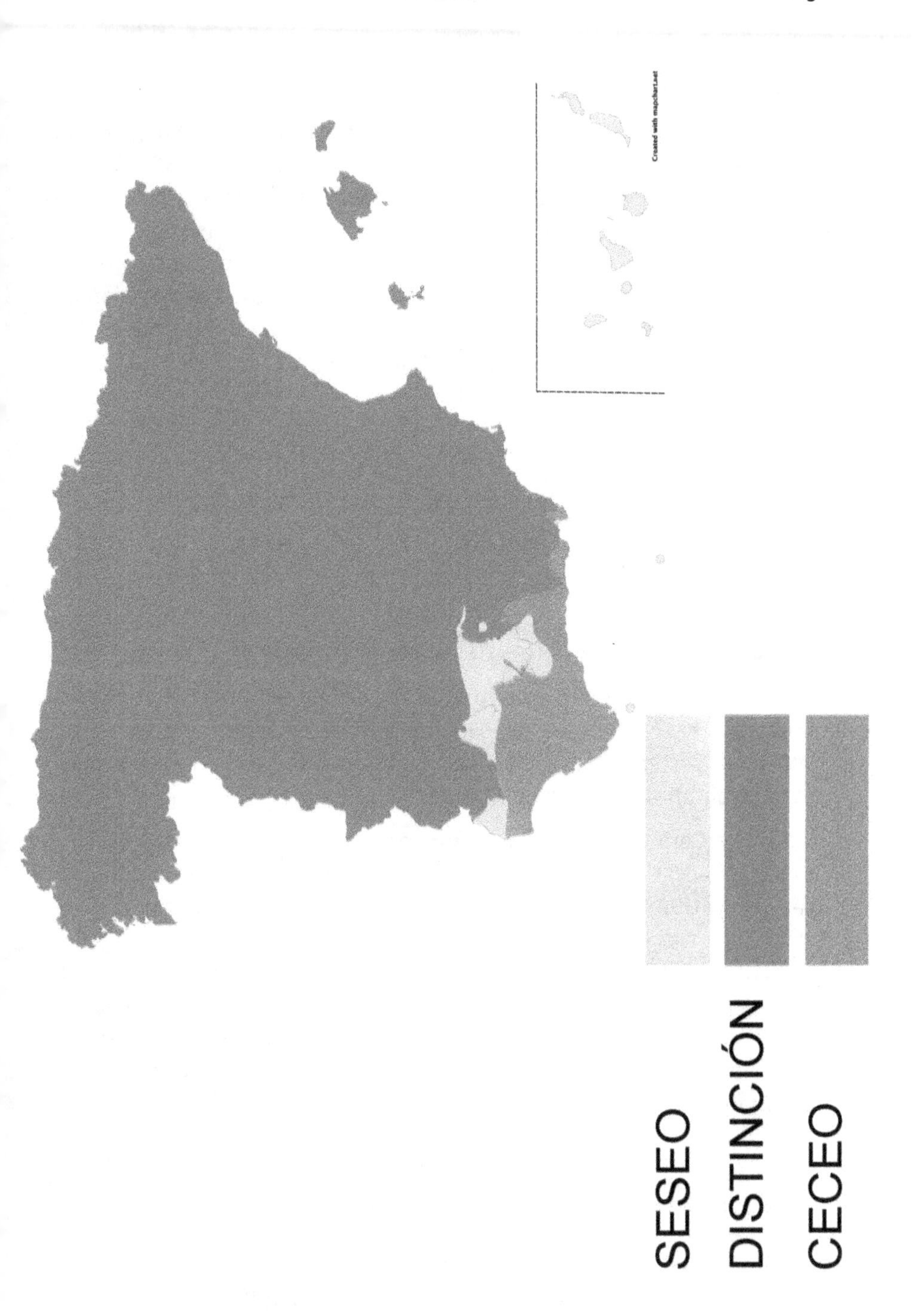

Map of Spain showing the geographic distribution of distinción, seseo and ceceo

▶ Weakening of syllable-final /s/

A very common phenomenon across the Spanish-speaking world, especially in the Caribbean, and the Southern Cone is the **ASPIRATION** or **ELISION** of the /s/ in coda position. Aspiration refers to a pronunciation in which the only obstruction in the vocal apparatus is at the glottis, resulting in a sound caused by the friction of the air passing through the glottis, which results in [h] rather than [s]. The total elimination or elision of the /s/ results in [Ø], i.e. the lack of a sound. This phenomenon is colloquially referred to as "eating one's s's".

Examples:

	Aspiration	Elision
las casas	[lah.'ka.sah]	[la.'ka.sa]
estás	[eh.'tah]	[e.'ta]

■ Variation in the pronunciation of liquids

Liquid sounds, consisting in Spanish of laterals and taps/trills (vibrantes). This category of consonants is quite susceptible to variation, which is attested in the tap as well as the trill, and there is also a case of neutralization of liquid consonants.

In the Caribbean, there is a phenomenon known as TRUEQUE DE LÍQUIDAS, or liquid-switching. This is the colloquial name for the process of **NEUTRALIZATION** of /l/ and /ɾ/ in syllable-final position. These sounds share several characteristics, differing only in their modes of articulation, so it stands to reason that they can be neutralized. There are two processes involved in this neutralization: **LATERALIZATION** (also known as **LAMBDACISM**), and **RHOTACISM**. The latter is much less common and more restricted than the former. Here are two examples:

Lateralization	**arma** ['al.ma]	**alma** ['al.ma]
Rhotacism	**arma** ['aɾ.ma]	**alma** ['aɾ.ma]

In addition to liquid-switching, there are also other types of regional variation in the pronunciation of /r/ (in any position), as well as syllable-final /ɾ/.

In the Caribbean (including Cuba, Puerto Rico, and the Dominican Republic), it is common to produce the trill /r/ with preceding glottal aspiration, represented [hr] o [h͡r]. In the Cibao region of the Dominican Republic (in the north), it is also possible to hear speakers that vocalize /ɾ/, turning it into a glide. With vocalization, the word **parte** (part) would be pronounced ['paj.te], and **mar** (sea) would be pronounced ['maj]. This is colloquially known as "speaking with the i".

An **ASSIBILATED** production of /r/ is often heard in Mexico, Central America, Paraguay, and the Andean region. This sound is transcribed as [ř] or [ɹ̥], and it involves a narrow stricture that produces the turbulent airflow characteristic of sibilance, a high-frequency whistling-like sound.

In some rural areas of Puerto Rico, there is also another variant of /r/, a uvular fricative, similar to the uvular allophone of /x/, [χ]. This variant tends to be voiced and is usually transcribed as [ʁ].

■ Variation in the pronunciation of the palatal stop/fricative

As explained in Chapter 9, there is considerable variation in the pronunciation of the consonant(s) that correspond to orthographic **ll** and **y**.

In Old Spanish, the orthographic **ll** corresponded to the phoneme /ʎ/, a voiced palatal-lateral approximant, while the **y** represented the voiced palatal stop or fricative /ɟ, ʝ/. Currently, in most of the Spanish-speaking world, these two phonemes have merged into one: /ɟ/. This merger involves the loss of the phoneme /ʎ/ from the inventory of sounds of these varieties of Spanish, a phenomenon called **YEÍSMO**. However, the distinction still exists in some regions of central and northern Spain, as well as parts of the Andean region of South America. This distinction is called **LLEÍSMO**.

In addition to yeísmo, there is another similar phenomenon found in speakers primarily from Argentina and Uruguay in which only one sound is used for both **ll** and **y,** called **ŽEÍSMO**, or the related **SHEÍSMO**. Žeísmo involves the use of the voiced palatal fricative consonant [ʒ], and sheísmo the voiceless palatal fricative [ʃ]. Over the last few decades, the voiceless variant has become increasingly common.

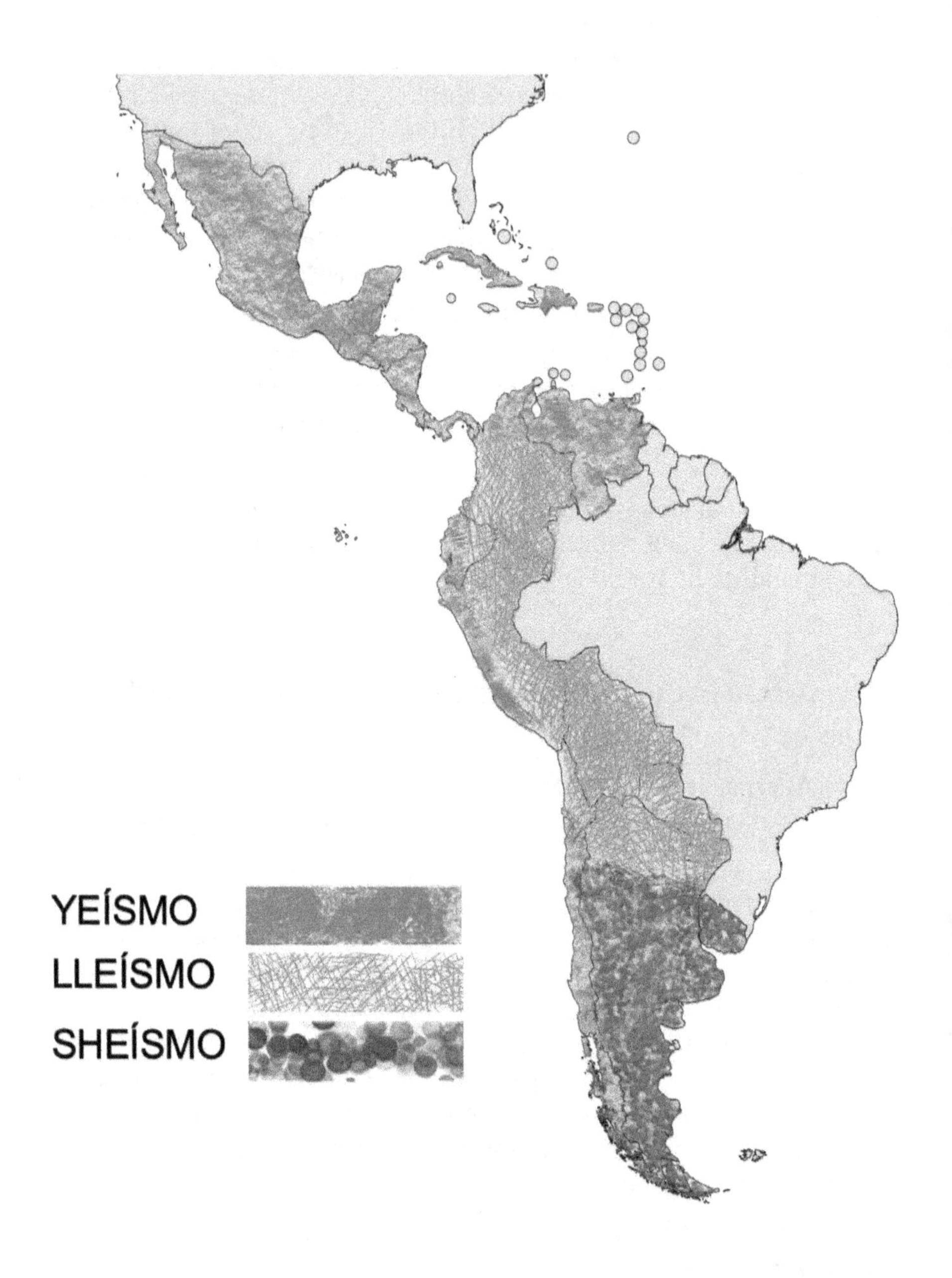

Map of Latin America showing the geographic distribution of yeísmo, lleísmo and sheísmo

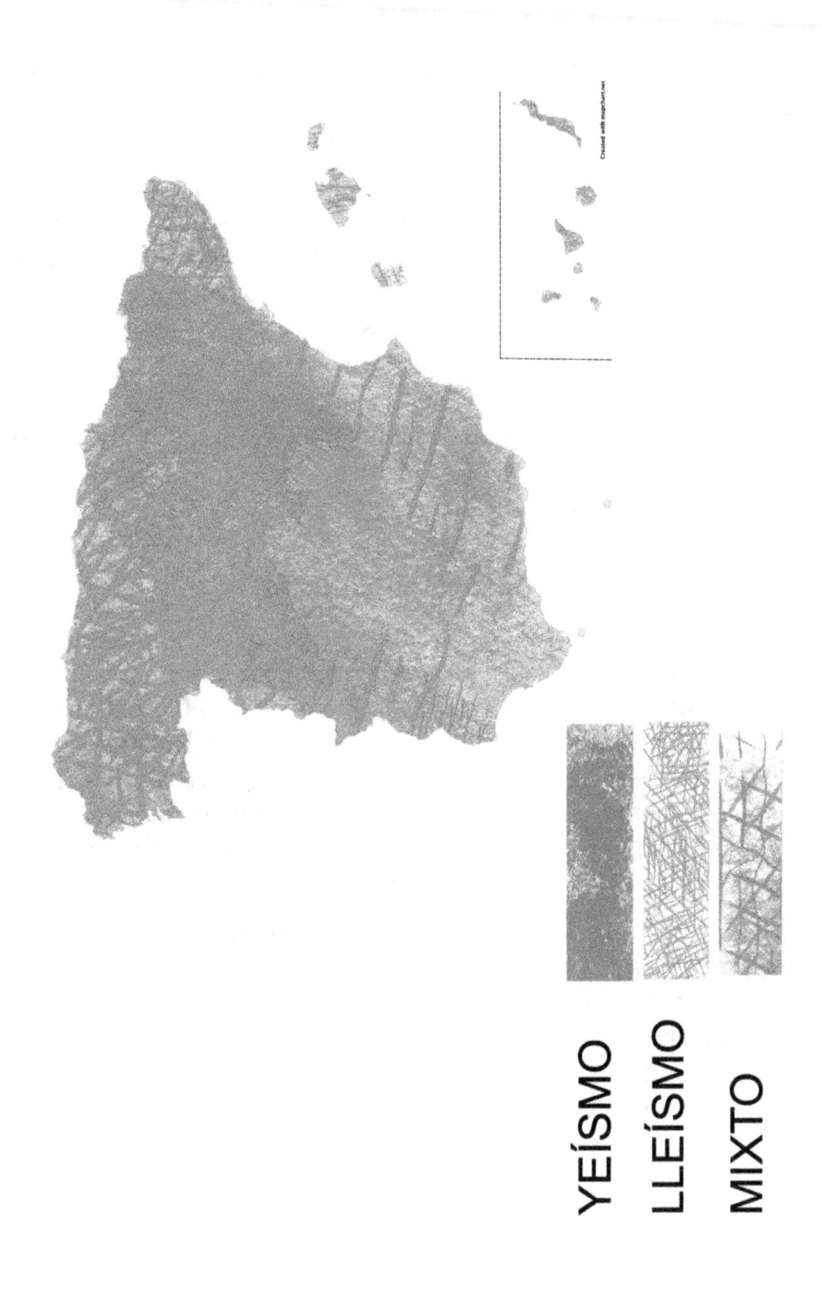

Map of Spain showing the geographic distribution of yeísmo and lleísmo, including areas that use both

■ Variation in the pronunciation of jotas (orthographic j)

The phoneme /x/ is associated with orthographic **j** as well as orthographic **g** before high vowels **e/i.** There is substantial variation in the pronunciation of this phoneme. The voiceless velar fricative variant [x] is used in various regions, such as for example in Mexico (except for the Yucatan), the Andean region (except Colombia and Bolivia), and in the Southern Cone (Chile, Argentina, Uruguay). In central and northern Spain, the voiceless uvular fricative variant [χ] is more common, whereas in other regions including Andalusia, the Canary Islands, the Caribbean, Central America (including the Yucatan peninsula), Colombia, and Bolivia, the most common variant is the voiceless glottal fricative, [h]. This is the same sound as the English **h**.

■ Variation in the pronunciation of vowels

In addition to the robust variation in consonant pronunciations across the Spanish-speaking world described above, there are also several cases of variation in vowel pronunciation. Some Puerto Rican and Mexican dialects have what is called variable **VOWEL RAISING**, which refers to a process affecting unstressed mid vowels /e, o/. In certain phonological contexts, the /e/ and /o/ raise and end up as a vowel closer to [i] and [u], respectively. This phenomenon results in the pronunciation of **llaves** as ['ʝa.βis] or **primo** as ['pri.mu].

Also, in the Andean region and in the center of Mexico, there is a variable phenomenon involving **DEVOICING**, **WEAKENING**, **SHORTENING**, and/or **ELISION** of unstressed vowels. In this process, the word **jitomates** could be pronounced [xi̥. to.'ma.te̥s] or [xi̥. to.'ma.ts]. In the Andes, this pronunciation is associated with social stratification, but in central Mexico it is used by the majority of people to some degree, although variably.

Questions

1. What is distinción? Seseo? Ceceo?
2. Considering your answer to the previous question, if you had to guess what the term "heheo" refers to, how would you respond?
3. How do you define neutralization?
4. Where is liquid-switching (the trueque de líquidas) commonly found?
5. What is lleísmo? Yeísmo? Where do they occur?
6. What is žeísmo? Sheísmo? Where do they occur?
7. What does it mean to "eat your s's"? Where does this occur most commonly?
8. What are the regional allophones of /x/? Where does each occur?

Exercises

1. **Give examples of five (5) minimal pairs that are distinguished only by phonemes /s/ and /θ/.**

2. **Using IPA symbols, transcribe the following minimal pairs three (3) times: 1st for a dialect with distinción, next for a seseante dialect, and finally, for a ceceante dialect.**

minimal pair	distinción	seseo	ceceo
asar/azar			
Asia/hacia			
masa/maza			
cocer/coser			
cello/sello			

3. **Transcribe each of the following phrases twice: once with characteristics of a Puerto Rican dialect, and then with characteristics of a Mexican dialect.**

   a. Vas a la fiesta, ¿verdad?

   b. Ramón nos dijo que está de acuerdo.

   c. Javiera es la mejor cantante que conozco.

4. **4. The list below shows several utterances along with their phonetic transcriptions. Try to guess where the speaker of each might be from.**

   a. “zona rural”: ['θo.na.ru.'ɾal]

   b. “ojos azules”: ['o.χoθ.a.'θu.eθ]

   c. “lugar determinado”: [lu.'ɣal.de.tel.mi.'na.ðo]

   d. “se llama José”: [se.'ʎa.ma.xo.'se]

   e. “hablar rapido”: [a'blaj.͡ɦra.pi.ðo]

   f. “derramar la leche”: [de.ɹ̥a.'mar.la.le.tʃi]

a.

b.

c.

d.

e.

f.

18

Phonetic transcription

You have seen examples of phonetic notation throughout this book, but it is a good idea to set down some basic rules here before we start to transcribe longer phrases or utterances (often using a recording of a speech act, a conversation, a speech, etc.).

A transcription is always done with a purpose, which determines the precision and the level of detail of this transcription. Sometimes it is necessary to do a narrow transcription, an exact and very thorough one showing all the details that can be heard (or seen using speech analysis software). On other occasions, it may be sufficient to provide a partial or broad transcription, which indicates only the most noticeable phonetic features of an utterance.

All phonetic texts are written between brackets [] to show that it is a phonetic transcription and not a phonemic one. These exist as well and are written between slashes //.

Before we can start transcribing a speech act, we must divide it into **PHONOLOGICAL PHRASES** that include all the sounds that are articulated between two pauses or periods of silence. The beginning and end are marked with the symbol #. Longer periods of silence, for example the end of a sentence or paragraph, can also be marked with ##.

Remember that a phonological phrase is treated as if it were a very long word and that speakers usually link the consonants at the end of a word with the vowel of the next word (if present) to create open syllables. This resyllabification or linking can also affect vowels, producing diphthongs and triphthongs.

In this book, we include the syllable breaks in the transcription. These are indicated with a period (.): [ma.no]. Note that there are no upper-case letters in a transcription, and no space between words unless there is a pause or period of silence. The stressed syllables are marked with the symbol ('): ['ma.no]. It is also necessary to remember that not all the words in a phonological phrase have a stressed syllable.

You must also avoid the temptation to use the same orthographic letters of written texts in the transcription. It is true that some of the phonetic symbols that we use in a transcription are identical to the letters of the alphabet, but there are exceptions. The letter **c** for example often sneaks into the phonetic transcription, but as an IPA symbol, it represents an unvoiced palatal stop consonant, which does not exist in Spanish. Therefore, if you see the letter **c** in writing, the appropriate IPA symbol will either be [s], [z] or [k], depending on the phonological context. Novices to phonetic transcription may also transcribe the letter **y** as [y] but the correct transcription is [i], [j], [ʒ], [ʝ],[ɟ] or [ʃ] depending on context. The letter **z** is [s] in IPA transcription, unless it precedes a voiced consonant. The grapheme **ch** is [tʃ], the grapheme **ll** can be [ʝ],[ɟ], [ʎ], [ʃ], or [ʒ], the grapheme **qu** is [k], and so on. It is important to keep these differences in mind, so as not to inadvertently create erroneous transcriptions by mixing up orthographic and phonetic symbols.

Only sounds are transcribed, meaning that silent letters like **h** or the **u** in words like **guerra** and **guía** are not included in the transcription.

Examples

Below, you can see some transcriptions of examples from the book.

Sigamos con el tema del placer. Desde el ángulo de la bioelectricidad, cuanto más abrupta sea la caída de potencial, mayor es la sensación de placer.

[si.'ɣa.mos.ko.nel̪.'t̪e.ma.ðel.pla.'seɾ##'des.ðe.'laŋ.gu.lo.ðe.la.'βjo.e.lek.t̪ri.si.'ðað#'kwan̪.t̪o.'ma.sa.'brup.t̪a.se.a.la.ka.'i.ða.ðe.po.t̪en.'sjal#ma.'ʝo.res.la.sen.sas.'jon.de.pla.'seɾ##]

Unos cinco mil cocaleros protagonizaron un bloqueo de la principal ruta de Bolivia, en contra de la proyectada instalación de tres bases militares en la convulsa región del Chapare. Los productores comenzaron el bloqueo de la vía que vincula el eje troncal del país conformado por los departamentos de La Paz, Cochabamba y Santa Cruz.

['u.no.'siŋ.ko.'mil.ko.ka.'le.ɾos#pɾo.t̪a.ɣo.ni.'sa.ɾo.nun.blo.'ke.o.ðe. la.pɾin.si.'pal.'ru.t̪a.ðe.βo.'li.βja#eŋ.'kon̪.t̪ra.ðe.la.pɾo.ʝek.'t̪a.ða.ins. t̪a.la.'sjon.ðe.t̪ɾes.'βa.ses.mi.li.'t̪a.ɾes#en.la.kom.'bul.sa.ɾe.'xjon. ðe.tʃa.'pa.ɾe##los.pɾo.ðuk.'t̪o.ɾes.ko.men.'sa.ɾo.nel.blo.'ke.o.ðe. la.'βi.a#ke.βiŋ.'ku.la.e.'le.xe.t̪ɾoŋ.'kal.ðel.pa.'is#koɱ.foɾ.'ma.ðo.poɾ.los. ðe.paɾ.t̪a.'men̪.t̪os.ðe.la.'pas#ko.tʃa.'βam.baj.san̪.t̪a.'krus##]

El profesor Pérez fue llevado ante el intendente municipal de la ciudad de Buenos Aires, Manuel Güiraldes, quien, poco después, lo designó laringólogo honorario del Teatro Colón que aún no se había inaugurado.

[el.pɾo.fe.'soɾ.'pe.ɾes.fwe.ʝe.'βa.ðo.an̪.t̪e.lin̪.t̪en.'ðen̪.t̪e.mu.ni. si.'pal#de.la.sju.'ða.ðe.βwe.no.'saj.ɾes#ma.'nwel.gi.'ɾal̪.des#'kjen#'po. ko.ðes.pwes#lo.ðe.si.'ɣno.la.ɾiŋ.'go.lo.ɣo.no.'ɾa.ɾjo#del.t̪e.'a.t̪ɾo. ko.'loŋ.ke.a.'u.no.se.a.'βi.aj.'naw.ɣu.ɾa.ðo##]

Glossary

English Term	Spanish Term	Definition
Affricate (sound)	**Africada**	The combination of a stop/ plosive and a fricative. The **ch** in **chin** is an affricate sound.
Agudas (words)	**Agudas (palabras)**	Words that have the stress on the last syllable.
Allophone	**Alófono**	Any of the phonetic variations and articulations of a phoneme. (= Sound)
Alveolar (sound)	**Alveolar**	Consonant sound in which the obstruction is produced with the tongue and the alveolar ridge. In English: **s**, **z**, **t**, **n**, **l**, and **d**.
Alveolar ridge	**Alvéolos**	Ridge or elevation between the upper teeth and the hard palate.
Americanism	**Americanismo**	A word or expression that originated or is used in the Americas.
Apical (sound)	**Apical**	Sound produced with the tip of the tongue, for example **[s̺]**.
Approximant (sound)	**Aproximante**	When an obstruction is too weak to produce friction, we call this approximation. Examples of approximants are [β], [ð], and [ɣ] in Spanish.

Aspiration	**Aspiración**	Use of the voiceless glottal fricative [h], an audible breath or burst of air, either in place of or in addition to another sound. In many contexts the English /p/, /t/ and /k/ are aspirated and become [pʰ], [tʰ], and [kʰ]. In Spanish, word-final /s/ is frequently aspirated, and produced as [h].
Assibilation	**Asibilación**	A sound change resulting in a sibilant consonant.
Assimilation	**Asimilación**	Phenomenon in which a sound assimilates or adopts one or more characteristics of a neighboring sound.
Autosegmental Metrical Theory	**Modelo métrico y autosegmental**	Intonational phonological framework that connects pitch with segments (syllables, phrase boundaries).
Bilabial (sound)	**Bilabial**	A sound produced with both lips, for example [m] or [b].
Boundary tone	**Tono de juntura o de frontera**	Rise or fall in pitch occurring at the end of an utterance.
Bunched r		The [ɹ] sound in American English produced by lifting both sides of the back of the tongue towards the upper molars.
Ceceo	**Ceceo**	The use of [θ] for both /θ/ (represented by the letters **c** (before **e** and **i**) and **z)** AND /s/ in some places in Andalusia, but also in parts of Puerto Rico and Central America.
Closed syllable	**Sílaba cerrada**	A syllable with a coda.

Coda	**Coda**	The coda (from Ital. `coda` = `cola, tail`) is a consonant or group of consonants after the nucleus of the same syllable.
Consonant	**Consonante**	A sound that encounters an obstruction in the vocal tract before exiting the mouth.
Continuant (sound)	**Continuante**	Sound produced with an uninterrupted airflow. Vowels are continuants, but so are consonants like /s/ or /n/, with partial obstructions.
Dental (sound)	**Dental**	A sound that is produced with tip of the tongue and the back of the upper incisors, for example **t** and **d** in Spanish.
Devoicing	**Desonorización**	Pronunciation of a typically voiced sound without vibration of the vocal cords.
Diacritical accent	**Tilde diacrítica**	A tilde (´) that is not used to mark the stressed syllable within a word, but to distinguish homographs (words with the same spelling, but different meanings and grammatical functions, for example **mi libro/ el libro es de mí**).
Digraph	**Dígrafo**	A group of successive letters whose phonetic value is a single sound, for example **ch**, **ll**, gu, **qu** and **rr**.
Diphthong	**Diptongo**	The combinations of **i** and **u** in the same syllable, as well as any combination of **a**, **e**, **o** + unstressed **i** or **u**.

Distinction	**Distinción**	The phonological distinction between /s/ and /θ/, for example, the differential pronunciation of **casa** ['ka.sa] and **caza** ['ka.θa]. Distinction is primarily restricted to Spain.
Distinctive features	**Rasgos distintivos**	Phonetic differences that result in phonological contrast, distinguishing the meaning of words, e.g., the difference between **papa** *(potato)* and **papá** *(dad).*
Elision	**Elisión**	The loss or deletion of a sound, for the example word-final /s/ or unstressed vowels.
Esdrujula	**Esdrújula**	Word with the stress on the third-to-last syllable.
Falling diphthong	**Diptongo decreciente**	Vowel sequence in which a glide [j] or [w] follows a full nuclear vowel, for example **ei**, **eu**, **ou**, **ai**, etc.
Family of sounds	**Familia de sonidos**	Series of sounds (allophones) that are used in different phonetic contexts, but that are part of the same phonological family. See also **Phoneme**.
Fricative (sound)	**Fricativa**	A consonant produced with a partial obstruction resulting in friction as the airflow passes through the vocal tract. The **s** in **see**, the **f** in **free** and the **s** in **pleasure** are fricatives.
Glide	**Deslizada**	See: **Semivowel**

Glottal (sound)	**Glotal**	A sound that is produced by the partial obstruction of the air flow through the glottis. The English [h], for example, is a glottal sound. (See: **Glottis**)
Glottal stop	**Golpe de glotis (oclusiva glotal)**	A complete closure of the glottis. (See: **Glottis**)
Glottis	**Glotis**	The part of the larynx consisting of the vocal cords and the opening between them.
Grapheme	**Grafema**	Each of the 27 letters and the 5 digraphs of the Spanish alphabet.
Hiatus	**Hiato**	Two adjacent vowels that occur in two separate syllables, e.g in **lío** and **paella**.
Indigenous influence	**Indigenismo**	Sounds, words, and lexical items pertaining to indigenous people of the Americas or taken from their languages.
Interdental (sound)	**Interdental (sonido)**	A sound that is produced with the tip of the tongue between the teeth. In English, there are two: the **th** of **bath** and **bathe**.
International Phonetic Alphabet	**Alfabeto fonético internacional (AFI)**	A set of symbols created and maintained by the International Phonetics Association to standardize the phonetic representation of all the sounds that exist in any language.
Labio-dental (sound)	**Labiodental (sonido)**	A sound that is formed with the lower lip and the upper teeth. The **f** and the **v** in English are labiodental sounds.
Lambdacism	**Lambdacismo**	See: **Lateralization**

Lateral (sound)	**Lateral (sonido)**	A sound in which the air flow is obstructed in the middle of the mouth and exits via both sides of the tongue and the mouth, e.g. /l/ in Spanish (and English).
Lateralization	**Lateralización**	The pronunciation of /ɾ/ like [l].
Linking	**Encadenamiento**	The connection of words across word boundaries within a phonetic phrase or utterance; resyllabification.
Liquid (consonant)	**Líquida (consonante)**	Both lateral and rhotic sounds have articulatory and phonotactic similarities in many languages, and therefore they are grouped together in this category.
Liquid-switching	**Trueque de líquidas**	Popular name for the neutralization of /l/ and /r/ at the end of syllables. See: **Rhotacism, lateralization**
Llana (word)	**Llanas (palabras)**	Words that have the stress on the penultimate (second-to-last) syllable.
Lleismo	**Lleísmo**	The phonemic distinction between the voiced palatal lateral approximant /ʎ/ and the voiced palatal stop /ɟ/, respectively written **ll** and **y**.
Manner of articulation	**Modo de articulación**	How a sound is pronounced; if it is oral, nasal, fricative, plosive, affricate, etc.
Nasal (sound)	**Nasal (sonido)**	Nasal sounds are produced when the velum is lowered and the air passes through and exits via the nasal cavity.

Nuclear stress	**Acento nuclear**	The main phrase-level stress, generally at the end of an utterance.
Nucleus	**Núcleo**	The central part of the syllable.
Nuclear vowel	**Vocal nuclear**	The vowel that forms the nucleus of a syllable.
Onomatopoeia	**Onomatopeya**	A word that imitates the sound of what it designates, for example **runrún.**
Onset	**Ataque**	A consonant or group of consonants preceding the nucleus of a syllable.
Open syllable	**Sílaba abierta**	A syllable without a coda, ending in a vowel.
Oral (sound)	**Oral (sonido)**	Oral sounds are produced when the velum is raised, which prevents the air from exiting through the nasal cavity, and instead directs it through the oral cavity. Most consonants in Spanish are oral.
Orthography	**Ortografía**	From Greek, meaning 'correct writing'; the system of symbols that exist in a language to represent sounds, words, and larger units in writing.
Palatal (sound)	**Palatal**	A sound produced with the tongue and the palate. In English, the sound **sh** in **ash** and **s** in **pleasure** are palatal consonants.

Phoneme	**Fonema**	The smallest unit of sound that can distinguish meaning. Phonemes are abstractions while allophones are their phonetic realizations. See also: **Family of sounds**
Phonetics	**Fonética**	Linguistic discipline that studies the acoustics, articulation, and perception of speech sounds.
Phonological phrase	**Frase fonológica**	All the words between two pauses or periods of silence in speaking or between punctuation marks (period, comma, semicolon, and others) in writing.
Phonology	**Fonología**	Linguistic discipline that studies sound patterns and systems. Reduces the inventory of sounds in a language to only those that are used to contrast meanings.
Pitch	**Tono**	The quality of a sound governed by the rate of vibrations producing it; the degree of highness or lowness of a tone.
Pitch accent	**Acento tonal**	Tone or pitch associated with a stressed syllable.
Place of articulation	**Punto de articulación**	Place or spot in the vocal tract where a consonant is articulated.
Primary stress	**Acento primario**	Main stress.
Pure vowel	**Vocal pura**	One of the vowels **a**, **e**, **i**, **o**, **u** as the nucleus of a syllable.

Rhotacism	**Rotacismo**	Neutralization process of liquid sounds in which /l/ is produced like [ɾ].
Rhyme	**Rima**	The part of a syllable consisting of the nucleus and the coda; everything that is not part of the onset.
Retroflex r	**r retrofleja**	The [ɹ] sound in American English produced by the retroflexion of the tip of the tongue towards the area between the alveolar ridge and the hard palate.
Rising diphthong	**Diptongo creciente**	Vowel sequence in which a glide [j] or [w] precedes a full nuclear vowel, for example **ie**, **ue**, **ia**, **io**, **ue** etc. or **ui**.
Schwa	**Schwa**	An unstressed mid central vowel represented by the symbol [ə] in the International Phonetic Alphabet. Many unstressed English vowels are reduced to [ə].
Secondary stress	**Acento secundario**	In between main stress and unstressed.
Semi-consonant	**Semiconsonante**	See: **Semivowel**
Semivowel	**Semivocal**	Vocalic sound in between a consonant and a vowel, produced when an unstressed high vowel occurs in the same syllable as a mid or low vowel, or a stressed high vowel. See also: **GLIDE**.

Seseo	**Seseo**	The lack of distinction between /θ/ (represented by the letters **c** (before **e** and **i**) and **z)** and /s/; the use of [s] for both.
Sheismo	**Sheísmo**	A variation of YEÍSMO; the use of the sound [ʃ] to pronounce the graphemes **ll** and **y**. See: **Yeismo**
Shortening	**Acortamiento**	A reduction in the duration of a sound.
Sobresdrujula	**Sobresdrújula**	Word that has the stress on the fourth syllable from the last.
Stop/plosive (sound)	**Oclusiva (consonante)**	A sound characterized by a complete obstruction of the air flow before it is released. The **p** in **pin**, the **t** in **tin** and the **k** in **kin** are plosives.
Stress	**Acento de intensidad** or **Acento prosódico**	The relative prominence of a syllable caused by increased articulatory effort and having contrastive meaning.
Stress timing	**Ritmo acentual**	Rhythmic pattern in which stressed syllables occur at regular intervals, and intervening unstressed syllables are shortened.
Stressed (syllable)	**Tónica (sílaba)**	The most prominent syllable, that which carries the lexical prosodic accent.
Suprasegmental (level)	**Nivel suprasegmental**	Features in an utterance such as intensity, rhythm, stress, pitch, intonation, etc.

Syllable timing	**Ritmo silábico**	Typical rhythmic pattern in Spanish based on the fact that all syllables have more or less the same duration, which means that the duration of a sentence or phrase depends on the number of syllables in it.
Synalepha	**Sinalefa**	The combination of a strong and a weak vowel within a phonetic phrase, between words, for example **la unión** [aw], **mi amigo** [ja], **la tribu amazónica** [wa]. See: **Diphthong**
Tilde	**Tilde**	Has two uses in Spanish: 1. the orthographic sign (´) 2. the orthographic sign (~)
ToBI (Tone and Break Indices)	**ToBI (Tone and Break Indices)**	Transcription system to represent and describe speech prosody and intonation.
Triphthong	**Triptongo**	The combination of semivowel + vowel + semivowel in the same syllable, for example in **Paraguay**.
Unstressed syllable	**Átona (sílaba)**	In Spanish, syllables are either stressed or unstressed. There is no secondary stress like in English.
Uvular	**Uvular**	A sound that is produced with the back of the tongue and the uvula.
Variation	**Variación**	The regional and socio-cultural differences within the same language.

Velar	**Velar**	A sound that is produced with the back of the tongue and the velum (soft palate). The **k** in `kite`, the g in `go`, and the **ng** in `king` are velar consonants.
Vibrant (sound)	**Vibrante (sonido)**	A sound that is produced by the vibration of the tongue against the alveolar ridge to produce the [ɾ] sound in **caro** or the [r] sound in **carro**. The vibration can be singular or multiple.
Voicing	**Sonoridad**	The vibration (or lack thereof) of the vocal cords.
Vowel	**Vocal**	A sound that comes out of the mouth without any obstruction.
Vowel raising	**Elevación vocálica**	A phonetic process affecting unstressed mid vowels in Spanish. In certain contexts, /e/ and /o/ are articulated with a higher tongue position and raise to [i] and [u]. Examples are the pronunciation of **llaves** as ['ɟ̞a.βis] or **primo** as ['pri.mu].
Weakening	**Debilitamiento**	The result of a reduction in articulatory effort, e.g. aspiration of /s/ at the end of words and syllables.
Yeismo	**Yeísmo**	A widespread pronunciation pattern representing the lack of phonemic distinction between the voiced palatal lateral approximant /ʎ/ and the voiced palatal stop /ɟ/, in favor of /ɟ/ for both **ll** and **y**.

Bibliography and further readings

- Clegg, J. Halvor, and Willis C. Fails. Manual de fonética y fonología españolas. Routledge, 2018.
- Hualde, José Ignacio. "El modelo métrico y autosegmental." Teorías de la entonación 155. 2003.
- Hualde, José Ignacio. The Sounds of Spanish. Cambridge University Press, 2005.
- Lipski, John M. "Socio-phonological variation in Latin American Spanish." The handbook of Hispanic sociolinguistics 72 (2011): 146.
- Morgan, Terrell. Sonidos en contexto. New Haven, CT: Yale University Press, 2010.
- Prieto, Pilar, and Roseano, Paulo, eds. Transcription of the Intonation of Spanish. München, Germany: LINCOM Studies in Phonetics. 2010.
- Real Academia Española (RAE). Ortografía de la lengua española. Espasa, 2010.
- Real Academia Española (RAE). Nueva gramática de la lengua española. Fonética y fonología. 2011.
- Schwegler, Armin, Juergen Kempff, and Ana Ameal-Guerra. Fonética y fonología españolas. John Wiley & Sons, 2018.
- Sosa, Juan Manuel, and Francesco D'Introno. La entonación del español: su estructura fónica, variabilidad y dialectología. Madrid: Cátedra, 1999.

Printed in the USA
CPSIA information can be obtained
at www.ICGtesting.com
JSHW011157151223
53707JS00003B/15